BEHAVE!
(AND WHY WE ALWAYS DO)

Communication *and* **Behavior:**
Your (DISC) Pattern

BEHAVE!

(AND WHY WE ALWAYS DO)

**Communication *and* Behavior:
Your (DISC) Pattern**

ABDUL TURKISTANI

First Edition

**Behave! (And Why We Always Do): Communication
and Behavior: Your DISC Pattern** / Abdul Turkistani

ISBN:
(paperback) 978-0-9997353-0-5
(hardcover) 978-0-9997353-1-2
(ebook) 978-0-9997353-2-9

Design by Elena Reznikova

*I dedicate this book to two most important
women of my life, whom I dearly love:*

*This book is my gift to my mom's soul, since without her
prayers I would not be able to write any words at all.
The book is also dedicated to my lovely wife, because without
her support I might never even have started
the book . . . much less finished it.*

Contents

Preface

Let me introduce myself. My name is Abdulbaset Turkistani. In everyday circumstances, I am an 'I-S'. I am inclined to see things in a 'glass-half-full' positive way and encourage others to do so, too. I love a good conversation! People are so interesting, you know? When disagreements arise (as we know they do in life), I don't want to feel left out! I believe it is more important to have harmony than to address the problem, so I jump more strongly into my 'S' side to create harmony and get everyone talking to each other again. My 'I' side is then convinced everything has been resolved and walks away, ignoring that a solution may not yet have been found.

What is this 'I-S'? Well, in the pages of this book, you will discover that! **I** and **S** are half of the **DISC** patterns of behavior I will be presenting and explaining to you.

To introduce myself more traditionally, I could have told you that I am a businessman and work as Training Manager in a petrochemical company where I lead the 34 employees of my department. I could also have told you that I and my family have for generations lived in Saudi Arabia, and that in my leisure time, I love to jog and travel internationally for vacations.

But if I had only introduced myself 'traditionally', you would have much less insight and understanding about who and how I am.

Yes, as you read these pages, you will discover that this traditional introduction of who I am is *much less revealing* of me than the first one with the **D, I, S** and **C** references I gave you—and which you do not yet understand. Rest assured, it is not some secret code!

In the next pages, I will be revealing how to interpret the patterns of your own behaviors and those of others. As I do so, I will be coming back to my own **D, I, S** and **C** references and those of some of my associates and clients (all names changed!) to illustrate how we use them to get along better, to get things done more effectively and quickly, to create more harmony and understanding in teams and groups—and hopefully inspire you to do the same.

It is my fondest wish that this information improves all your relationships and interactions at home and out in the world!

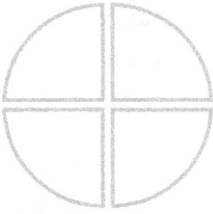

Introduction

NO MATTER what type of life we are living, I can guarantee you that your life is about relationships. Certainly, we have relationships with nature and technology, with our governments and our institutions. The types of relationships we have seem countless. But the most important—and challenging—relationships we have are with other individuals and with ourselves.

That is what makes it so very astonishing that—despite millennia of *understanding clearly* what makes the human beast tick—we don't teach a specific course in any of our schools about understanding human behavior. We don't learn how to understand our own behaviors! We certainly don't learn to understand or adapt to those of other individuals.

This book is my attempt to remedy that situation, in the hope that amongst all the readers it may attract, teachers will latch onto its message, its explanations and its illustrations and pass them on to their students.

If you are the parent of a child who has reached adulthood, you witnessed firsthand the pain of your child's lack of understanding about how to get along with each and every child in his various classes and social interactions. A child will always think it's 'his fault' if things go badly around him. And that is just not so.

If you are the heart of a household, such as a grandparent or parent, you know that each member of your family presents a slightly (or radically!) different behavior style. If your family members' style is much different from yours—not to mention its opposite—you have probably had situations in which you are hard-pressed to create dialogue, harmony, agreement or cooperation.

If you are out in the world of work, you are amongst adults whose behavior styles seem to be irrevocably cemented into them. The fact is that when you can't get along with people you work with, your very livelihood or career might truly be in jeopardy. And it doesn't need to be that way.

Whatever your age, you are surely amongst people who never seem to get along with anyone, as well as with others who seem to be generally popular. Why is that?

Well, this book is my response to that latter question. Don't skip any chapters. Don't skip any sections. If I ask you to do a quick quiz or exercises, please do them. I trust that by the end of the book, your question "Why is that?" will be answered.

Chapter 1

What Makes Relationships So Difficult?

> *"No man is an island, entire of itself;*
> *every man is a piece of the continent."*
> JOHN DONNE, ENGLISH POET, 1624

RELATIONSHIPS CAN provide us with a deep support and inner strength, and build us up emotionally so that we feel we are being our best person. Other relationships suffer from the start from contradictory hard and fast expectations and demands that neither party can meet, and all exchanges are fraught with conflict and discontent.

While it is certainly true that each of us has some terrifically happy and loving relationships, we all have some difficult ones. 'Difficult' is of course defined differently from one relationship to

1

another. Sometimes the difficulty is just in the imbalance—one person always demands to win the argument or have things his way, or one person listens more or talks more than the other. Occasionally the difficulty is deeper and puts a job at risk, or threatens the cohesion of a marriage or family. And then, there are simply those people that from our first encounter we say, "I just don't like him." We don't know why, but that's our initial feeling about that person, and we cannot seem to shake the impression off.

Why so many of us are experiencing difficult relationships and what to do about it is the subject of this book. While it is a shame that—like earning and managing money—understanding people is not something taught in our schools, you can start here, in these pages.

We have all grabbed our heads in dismay at some point in our lives and asked these questions:

Why is it so hard to figure other people out?
Why can't they figure me out?
Why can't they be more like me?

Here are some ways in which people simply are not alike, and the relationship presents real communication challenges:

- You are a social, gregarious parent with a shy, quiet child. How do you connect with that child, and enjoy more open, two-way interactions with her?

- Your younger sister is a wild child, willing to try everything once and to break the rules to do so. How do you, her rule-following, parent-obeying older brother worried about her getting into trouble (or worse) not only share your concerns with her so that she listens, but get her to behave more 'like you'?

- The boss is supposed to be a leader, right? Unfortunately, in our workplaces that is not always the case. What can you do, as that boss's supervised employee, to help the team do your jobs right . . . without going over his head or making him look bad?

- Physicians are quite the authority figure around the world. Your father is quite ready to believe what the doctor says without question. You, however, are skeptical of all authorities' statements and believe in doing your own research. When your father's health condition gets worse, how do you get the know-it-all doctor to hear what you have to say from your own research . . . in defense of your father's health and very life?

- Both you and your spouse have been thinking that you are on the verge of divorce. What a painful situation! You seem to communicate at cross purposes. You seem to have contrary expectations of each other's role in the relationship. Perhaps sharing and applying the information in this book is a far better solution than divorce . . .

- As the head of your household, you are quite willing and able to take charge and make the decisions for everyone. You are totally flustered by your daughter's tearful protest that you are not taking everyone else's opinions into account. What is a father to do?

I believe in all types of relationships the top two problems that make things difficult between and amongst people are

1. miscommunication / lack of communication
2. unmet expectations

In the above examples, the individuals had difficulty communicating with each other. And that is primarily, I think, because of the second problem which is that *we expect everyone else to think, behave and react, just like we do*. When they don't (and believe me—they won't), we are totally lost!

Of all the relationships we have with other people, unfortunately, too many of us can count on a single hand the number of perfectly harmonious and mutually beneficial relationships we have. We need more great relationships!

Interacting with other individuals is simply part of our lives. While not all of us enjoy being alone, those of us who seek it may only truly be 'alone' when we are in some of our deepest prayers or meditations, or in our deepest sleep. All the rest of the time, life is about relationships—and there's no getting around this fact.

By simple observation from our youngest years, we all know that relationships with other individuals are not always simple and easy. They are not always loving and safe. Nor are they always trusting and honest. But we also recognize that there are people we seem to get along with right away with ease, and we wonder why all our relationships are not that easy.

It is frustrating for us to see that people are 'different from me' and not know how to be heard, how to act, how to be understood . . . even within our own family.

Because we have no other roadmap, we carry this relationship confusion over into our organizations and our nations. Not all businesses or organizations who look like natural partners on the outside can manage to create a partnership that works from the inside. Not all nations who seem to have shared goals and interests manage to work together to achieve them. Somehow, the relationships just don't seem to work. Conflict seems to be the rule; communication seems elusive.

We team up with others on an equal footing, or we are the team leader. We manage a family as the head of the household, or we are one of those living within a framework the head of household has created. We have a large network of friends, associates and extended family that we socialize with regularly—or we are homebodies. Whatever the case, each of us has to interact with other people at some time or another. We follow a leader, or we are that leader.

In our homes, communities, during travel, and in our workplaces—interactions with other individuals are every day occurrences, and we need to manage them much better. That means we first need to know and manage ourselves first, and we really do not!

In the different hierarchies of relationships, there are different expectations of behavior. Modifying our behavior to suit the relationship or the circumstances is not always as intuitive as it might seem, and I believe that is because we have confusion about the *patterns of human behavior*. It is also because we expect everyone to be like us when that is so rarely true.

We unrealistically expect everyone to behave like us.
Life itself is our reality check.

Unpredictability Will Be Banished

Not seeing patterns in the behaviors of others makes people <u>seem</u> unpredictable to us. Feelings and emotions and moods are the first reasons. Not all of us wake up in the same mood day after day after day. There seems to be no rhyme or reason, no pattern to those moods. One of my clients said he has (so far) identified seven very different moods in his business partner and never knows how to position himself in the face of those changing moods! This is a clue that others don't know either! People you are in contact with on a daily basis are put on the spot to adapt to your new 'mood of the day', with no tools for doing so comfortably. Not understanding the other individual's 'patterns' as discussed in the introduction is a big reason that our relationships and people's behaviors may seem unpredictable.

In these pages, you will move from a place where everyone's behavior *seems unpredictable,* to a place of *predictability.* To a better understanding of what is motivating individuals to behave as they do. It will give you a big advantage in creating, fixing or improving relationships you have . . . and in knowing yourself more deeply than before.

Chapter 2

Why Strive for Better Relationships and Interactions?

RELATIONSHIPS ARE everywhere, every day. Inescapable.

If you scan the bookshelves of your bookstore or library, or surf the Internet with the question "why improve relationships?", you are probably going to come across a challenge. There are lots of books and articles out there to tell you *how* to improve any type of relationship you're having problems with. You'll also find that most of them are about marriage or couples' relationships. It seems that writers forget that we have parent/child, boss/employee, vendor/client, leader/follower, public/private relationships, etc. (just to name a few). There are very few books, though, that tell you *why* it is such a great idea to do some work to improve relationships of all the types that exist! Why improve? Why make the effort? That's a big question!

I believe you need to know all the reasons for which you are embarking on improving relationships with the people in your life before you can ever expect success in doing so. Face it—if you are not personally motivated to create and see change yourself, and for very clear reasons, nothing's going to happen.

I have observed that when people know *why* they have set a goal (I call it 'the goal behind the goal'), then the ways and means to achieve it magically appear and the goal is more easily attainable.

Take a moment right now and think firstly about those diffi-cult relationships you have. These are relationships which cause you grief or some other unpleasant feeling day after day or month after month on quite a regular basis. Nothing you do seems to change things. Secondly, now also think about the happy and loving relationships you have, which only occasionally have a few rough spots. For example, why do you and your sister argue once a year? Why not every day . . . or never? What is it that creates that rough spot once a year? As you think about these two types of relationships that we all have, why do you personally wish to improve either? Don't give someone else's reasons, only your own. Write them down somewhere. Do that right now. List all the reasons you can think of for the first type of relationship, as well as the second type.

Benefits

Those reasons you have just listed are really the *benefits* you will enjoy when you embark on improving your relationships. In addition to those personal reasons you have just listed, I can share with you benefits that I have observed in my practice.

One of the first benefits of improving your own understanding of how other people act and communicate is your new ability to *'translate,'* so to speak, or interpret one person's context to another individual who is propelled by a different behavior style. In my work, I teach bosses and supervisors how to do this and they always benefit greatly from doing so. However, keep in mind that they are not the only ones on the front line to make improvements. You are responsible for your own relationships. Any little positive change you can make will improve your interactions.

You are responsible for your own relationships.

Your Health

Another of the astonishing benefits people I work with experience when they make serious steps towards improving their relationships is in *recovering their own physical and emotional health.* Does that sound strange to you? It should not! When relationships don't go well, it creates emotional and mental stress within us, and that stress goes on to wreak havoc with our body's health.

Don't assume that it is only your closest family relationships that can play games with your health. Anyone you spend time with but do not get along well with—a spouse, a child, a coworker, or a boss—is hazardous to your health! Here is a sample of how:

> A man got a new job and he saw his manager as rude, abrupt, dictatorial and simply unprofessional—a bully, really. He felt a palpable emotional dread any time the manager came around to observe his work group. This manager was never pleased with any work, was out to insult everyone (including him) every chance he got. He felt disrespected and attacked by his manager, but didn't know what to do except do his best. He started to hate going to work, got headaches during the day, lost his appetite and energy. He was seriously thinking about simply looking for another job elsewhere.

Being Heard

In our busy lives and our busy, noisy world, people's complaint about many of their relationships is that no one listens anymore. Too many people are walking around feeling invisible, feeling that no one listens to them, feeling that no one hears them when they speak. That no one knows who they really are. People can feel that no one knows 'where they are coming from'—their position in the world is not understood.

A behavior style is your context; it's where you are coming from! Keep reading and you will grasp the four basic contexts called **DISC** that people might 'come from.' You will learn how to hear people, fully interact with them *right in their context*, so that they feel valued.

Thus, the second significant benefit people report to me once they have 'fixed' or improved a relationship that had been bothering them is the huge spike in a feeling of *acceptance, being heard* and *being understood* by the other. Conflict melts away. Confusion lessens. Communication is more comfortable.

When you do not know another person's behavior style (and we will get to that very quickly), you also have little understanding of how he communicates. Communication is not only verbal, but is shared through body language, and through how an individual listens . . . or does not.

When you understand an individual's behavior style, you have a much better grasp of how he communicates with others. You can adapt a little bit better to what that individual expects, create comfort for him—and see how it is reciprocated.

Most parents identify a communication disconnect at some point with their child. On the child's side, suddenly that mother and father don't understand him at all, suddenly mother and father never listen to her! On the parents' side of things, they'll say that suddenly their daughter is withdrawn, or suddenly their son goes wild and shouts all the time. If that sounds like most teenagers, you are right, but it can actually happen at any point in a growing child's development . . . and in a parent's scrambling to 'keep up and understand' what the child needs.

Support

Related to the previous benefit, when you understand other people's expectations and communication styles, the third benefit of improving relationships is *the support you feel from others and can appropriately offer to other people.*

Support comes in many forms. It might be that you now have someone to go to when you need a helping hand, and likewise, you immediately see when a person needs your help—because you understand his context, his behavior and communication styles better. Support can mean that you see when the other's context is not understood, and he is floundering—you can step in and 'translate' what is needed or what is happening into that person's own terms.

> You know from your understanding of various behavior styles (and that understanding will come quite soon in these pages!) that your coworker and your boss are like oil and water on any project. You go ahead and let your boss dictate the project parameters, then you are able to turn around and help your coworker understand the task, organize it into his preferred way, and feel comfortable about his contribution.

Even when you are by no means in charge, you can serve as 'translator' between two styles of behavior.

Bring to mind your most difficult relationship. Now think, too, of the 3 people closest to you (or with whom you spend the most time). How would you benefit if you understood and communicated with each one of these people more harmoniously, and miscommunicated less?

Workplace Success

I've worked with companies that come to me to 'obtain' greater productivity and efficiency from the people they already employ. Managers and supervisors are witnesses every day to the fact that people don't always get along with each other. When these are the exact people that the company needs urgently to work together productively and harmoniously to reach company goals, that presents a problem. Managers also keep the quality of their employees' interactions and communication style with each other in mind at performance review time. Most managers are simply not willing to promote individuals who refuse to get along or who refuse to learn and grow. This book is your guide to learning how to get along better with everyone at your workplace (and why others may not be getting along with you), while you learn more and more about yourself and them. People who get promoted are good at reading people, working harmoniously, doing their part to achieve a shared goal, accepting responsibility as needed—that's a fact of business life.

I hope this work of understanding what makes people tick expands your achievement of a happier, calmer, more productive, healthier life for yourself.

Are There Any Drawbacks?

In my experience, the biggest drawback to improving your relationships in the home, in the workplace or in the greater world is quite simply that you don't understand what it is that you are trying to fix! Thus, the first drawback is context—you need a source of knowledge about human behavior. I provide that to you in this book.

How could there be any drawbacks to improving relationships, you ask? Well, there are. The main thing is that people are creatures of habit. We all are, no matter what you might say, driven more by our habits than any conscious decision. And what are habits but . . . more patterns? It is those very habits, which researchers believe determine over 70% of our actions every day, which we need to change in order to improve our relationships.

Habits are just patterns.

Habits are so ingrained that we believe they are hard or impossible to change. If you have ever known anyone who needs to lose weight for the first time, you can easily name the ingrained (past) habits that need to be changed—doing exercise, when the individual has never done any before; eating considerably less, when the person has never controlled the amount of food eaten; choosing to eat totally different foods, when the individual has never concerned himself with such things. Those are three huge habits that need changing, and there are certainly others for many people when they lose weight. Why do people fail? Because they refused to change their old habits for new ones.

We encounter the same drawbacks to improving relationships. Our own behavior and communication style need to be slightly repositioned—if only for a brief moment—in order to improve our interactions with people of other styles. That slight readjustment is a new habit. It will mostly be brief, such as the span of a brief meeting with a team member, or a short chat with your child before going out to work. But oh, how we resist changing from an old to a new habit!

My goal with this book is to help you understand what makes people tick, and to illustrate to you where challenges may arise in yourself as well as in other people. Only then can you make the kinds of adjustments that improve interactions. Only then, with your greater understanding of people's behavior styles, can you improve your personal and working relationships with them.

I'm here to tell you that you can do it! It all starts with more complete and exact *knowledge* of the four primary human behavior patterns or styles called **DISC**. You need some facts about human behavior styles before you know how to change any habit. That's coming up.

Chapter 3

Recognizing Yourself:
The First Steps

"Know thyself."
ANCIENT GREEK SAYING

THE GREEK teacher and writer Plato said in several different ways that to 'understand yourself would enable you to have an understanding of others as a result'. Indeed, philosophers of all ages have said something to this effect. That is what I'm proposing for you to do in this and the following chapters: through an understanding of behavioral patterns, you can understand yourself, in order to better understand others. When relationships aren't as harmonious as you wish they were, you can go about improving them by learning what makes others tick. But as the ancient philosopher said, "Know thyself" first.

Not everyone seems to act in predictable ways? That is because *not everyone is like you*. But what are your own behaviors, styles and patterns? It is difficult to say, 'others are different', when you cannot accurately describe yourself.

Whose job is it to improve a rocky relationship? I have to say it: It is 100% your job. It all starts by <u>understanding yourself</u> better first. And please do not protest to me that you know yourself very well. If your relationships are not working (or if even one of them is in distress), you don't know yourself well enough. It is as simple as that.

Do you exhibit a predictable pattern of behaviors?
Indubitably, yes!
The trick is knowing what that pattern is.

Since childhood you have displayed some dominant personality traits (also called character traits). When my family says, *"That's so typical of Abdul!"*, they are referring to one or more of my dominant traits or predictable (for me) behaviors. We can all do something like this with our best friends, our own children or spouse, our business partners, or well-known public figures.

Our repeated behaviors are part of what make us predictable to others, for better or for worse. It is time to be able to do this with yourself and your own traits.

An Informal Assessment First

You think you know yourself so well. It is time to prove that to yourself. Write out a description of yourself right now—before reading about any of the behavioral style chapters coming up and without me giving you any guidelines as to how to do that.

Use individual descriptive words or phrases. I suggest that you write down all your thoughts, and keep the notes you take close by so that you can refer to them as you read the four behavioral style chapters. Do that now.

A Guided Approach Next

Now take a new sheet of paper. I will guide you a bit this time in describing your behavior style.

Without making any type of 'good/bad' judgments, list your most prominent character traits and your most frequent or predominant feelings and behaviors for any period of your life

1) in which everything is going quite smoothly,
   according to an expected routine
2) in which everything is going badly, with lots
   of dilemmas, problems to deal with, and crises
   erupting all around you.

If you are honest with yourself, you will probably note two very different sets of behaviors, feelings, actions and reactions.

For #1, you'll say, "I never follow the rules; I just can't do it; I don't like rules or need them."

For #2, you'll shift into admitting, "I pull the rule book out and help people out of the mess by following tried-and-true processes."

Now consider your closest siblings and your parents for the same two types of situations—the first when everything is going smoothly and according to usual routines, and the second when disaster breaks out all around them. How do each of those individuals close to you act, react, behave and feel in each of those two opposite types of circumstances? Do you see some sort of shift in most of them?

Our Environment

After doing those two exercises, we must additionally admit that each of us is largely the product of the family raising us, as well as of the society we were raised in.

1) write down the dominant beliefs, traditions, expected behaviors that came from the family who raised you.

2) write a list of the character traits you believe describe a fair majority of individuals in the society (country, nation) in which you were raised and are living. If that seems difficult, just imagine that you

are overseas, and a foreigner there asks how you would describe your countrymen.

My guess is that this was a difficult set of exercises for you to complete! In the next few chapters I will reveal ways in which these very same exercises can become easier. As you learn about patterns of behavior of individuals and in yourself, describing your actions and reactions in various circumstances and with a range of people will become easier and easier to predict. In fact, people themselves will become predictable to a greater degree, and you will be able to momentarily modify your behavior to create a beneficial interaction with them.

Putting Things into Some Order

Let me give you here a clue as to how to understand people's behaviors through one very simple observation. I will dive more deeply into this in the **DISC** chapters, but this is your sneak preview into people's patterns of behavior!

Go back into all the words you wrote. Did you write anything about _tasks_ or activities? Anything about being around _people_ or relationships with them? If not, now ask yourself, and answer, this question:

1) Do I most prefer (am I most comfortable and at ease) dealing with tasks and things, or would I be happier dealing and being with people?

I ask you this question because people have a strong tendency to fall into one of these two observable habits, which the above questions reveal to you. Here are the habits, so see which *one* describes you best:

→ **Task**-orientation, activity-orientation OR
→ **People**-orientation, relationship-orientation

Although everyone is around people and everyone performs some kinds of tasks, almost everyone prefers one or the other— either to stay with doing tasks because you are most comfortable doing things, or leave the 'doing' to others in favor of being around people.

> If you look back at our story in chapter 2, you start to see that the dictatorial manager was not people-oriented whatsoever! Chances are that he had a very, very strong *task-orientation*. If you look at the employee, you might guess that the employee *expected* more *people-orientation* from his manager—and did not get this from him. The employee *expected* the boss to be more like him, but he was not! In this very simple and short analysis, you can see just one way that these two individuals are different, and the types of shift in their respective behaviors they might need to make in order to get along better when they need to interact. The task-oriented manager would need to temporarily shift into more of a people-attentive behavior. The employee, with his people-oriented expectations, would need to move for a brief moment into more of a task-orientation to connect better with his boss.

These habits are part of each of the **DISC** styles in specific ways you will soon see. That is all I will say until I have presented all four of the **DISC** behavioral styles. Then I will guide you in understanding how to make shifts in your own usual behavior to temporarily adapt to the other person's style, so that you get along a bit better with each other.

Formalizing Things with an Online Self-Assessment—DISC

The assessment I use—called the **DISC** Profile—is your best first step to knowing *yourself* better and seeing *yourself* within patterns of behavior. It has been used for decades and decades, and scientifically proven to provide accurate results.

A **DISC** assessment uses your responses to various situations to show how you typically respond to ordinary daily events or tasks and interactions, to challenges or emergencies. You can take the assessment online and all you do is select one of several provided responses. The result shows how you respond to or influence others, respond to rules and procedures, etc., as we will clearly see in the **DISC** chapters.

All the words you have written down to describe yourself–which are your *behavioral tendencies*—will fall into one of four styles or patterns that today are called **DISC**. The gentleman I described in chapter 2 (with the dictatorial manager) would discover that he and that manager have opposite styles. As you read the coming chapters on the four **DISC** styles, you will understand in greater detail why he was so confused about the manager, and what else each one can do to get along better. In fact, it is in both of their interests to make slight shifts in their usual styles of behavior—the employee, for his own comfort and the manager to allow the employee to work more productively (more on that after the **DISC** chapters).

In a nutshell, you need to recognize one fact as your starting point:

Not everyone is like you, but you can still get along!

That is the perhaps rather obvious (but too often forgotten) place we all need to start in our journey 1) to understand our own behavioral tendencies, 2) to understand the styles of other individuals, and then 3) to put it all together to understand how to get along with each other despite those observed differences.

'Different' is not bad! 'Different' is just one of the many ways life among people is so very interesting!

After you read this entire book, you can certainly do a shortened or quick **DISC** assessment from any number of online sources. They are a good place to start in your ongoing efforts to understand yourself and position yourself in relation to others' behavioral styles. If you would like to do a full assessment, you can surely contact me, and I will help!

Refer to my resources at the end of the book, or simply go online and google "full DISC profile assessment."

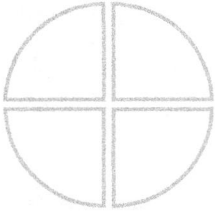

Chapter 4

If We Are So Unique, Where Do Those Patterns Come From?

I SPOKE of patterns in my introductory comments. How do we know another living being is human? Odd question!

Human DNA is a pattern. Having one of the human blood types (of which there are only a handful), skin, hair or eye colors also represent patterns of which there are only a few. It is the patterns of body shapes and functions—one torso, two arms, two legs, neck and head—that help us recognize each other as human beings, and also that we are 'put together' in a pattern that has been repeated billions of times!

Other patterns exist in the way we move and use our bodies. It is called body language. Some body language is shared amongst a huge number of societies. For instance, when the face shows happiness or sadness, fear or anger, or repulsion or surprise—numerous peoples around the world understand what is written on that face. Did you know that people born blind also express these emotions with exactly the same facial expressions as their sighted fellowman? That is truly universal! Patterns.

I read somewhere that humans display 'only' about 900 different facial features and the billions of us on the planet each have our own personal *combination* of these features to make it seem like we have a unique face. But if that number is correct, we have more like a 'one in a million' face! Even though 900 seems like a large number to create any kind of pattern, it is possible to do so. That it is possible has allowed brilliant minds to create a viable facial recognition software (which is largely, but not only, used by governments around the globe) and optical/retinal identification software.

There is one other pattern that is a bit different from the ones I have just named. Among people around the globe, we share four searches. They have nothing to do with our bodies, but with our motivations and desire to fit in and find our true place in the world. They have nothing to do with our culture or our education. Whether conscious or subconscious, there are rarely exceptions to these patterns. Observation on your part will prove this out. All people seek these four things—the pattern is universal.

1. All people seek a degree of personal control over their environment.
2. All people seek some degree of approval and appreciation, even love from other individuals.
3. All people seek a measure of safety, security of their body, and of people or things they feel attached to.
4. All people seek a spiritual connection or oneness with the greater family of man.

Human behavioral styles similarly follow patterns, which experts have found ways to identify and categorize to make our lives easier for us. With a willingness to understand these patterns, I believe, we can ensure that we not only seek but find control, approval, security and connection.

While there are probably thousands of feelings (or at least many words and phrases that refer to feelings and emotions), and a large number of descriptions for our various behaviors, experts have distilled down these huge numbers into (in the case of **DISC**) four categories or styles of behavior which can help us each position ourselves, as well as position others we work and live with.

Once we have positioned ourselves or others based on observation of behavioral patterns, we gain the knowledge necessary to decide whether we need to make some changes in our behaviors, actions or reactions or not.

Behavior is contextual.

Keep in mind that there are no all-good or all-bad behavioral traits until the whole context has been identified. The context (the current situation) becomes, thusly, part of the pattern that you need to identify. A trait of yours that is very beneficial to you in one context may be detrimental in another. We'll look at that, too.

Formalized Assessments and Profiles

Human behavior is nearly 95% predicable because of patterns. You may protest that you do a lot of things 'spontaneously' and thus unpredictably. Not so! Your very spontaneity 'trait' is a predictable pattern. Because of human routines, habits and patterns, there are virtually no 'spontaneous individuals' out there in the world.

Scientists and researchers have always known about patterns, and a lot of what they do or where they start in their studies is about a recognized pattern. Human behavioral patterns are no exception.

The first 'scientific' personality assessments began to be developed in the 1920s. Swiss psychiatrist and psychoanalyst Carl Jung's research about 'ordinary people's emotions' was some of that early research. Dr. William Moulton Marston's research work began around the same time as well. (You may have heard of him as the inventor of the polygraph or lie detector, or as the creator of the popular comic book character Wonder Woman). He was a multi-talented, brilliant man, looking scientifically into how a shift in normal emotions could lead people to change their behaviors, and then to how a new situation or context could again change a person's behavior. His understanding of patterns led him to identify just four <u>behavioral styles</u> within which all people's behavior fell, in some combination. He saw that, without exception, people's behavior fell into either a *D*/Dominance, an *I*/Influence, an *S*/Steadiness, or a *C*/Conscientiousness pattern. Thus, the four styles we call **DISC**.

As is typically the case for any new technology (and these tools definitely qualify as 'a technology'), it was the military or armed forces back then that further developed them specifically to help in selecting and assigning personnel to the best work group or type. The premise was that certain behavioral styles are more suited to certain types of jobs than others. Today, any business doing such assessments uses them in exactly the same way—to correctly recruit new personnel for job openings they have to fill, and to make sure their staff is 'behaviorally assigned' to the right sort of job function or tasks.

The **DISC** assessments start with simple questionnaires. You are asked a question, you choose an answer which represents your 'typical response', and move to the next question. In the questionnaires, there are no right or wrong answers—not ever!

There are a number of profiles on the market today, but for its completeness and accuracy and for its broad application to so many people, the **DISC** assessment is my top choice. With its 4 distinct 'styles', anyone can understand the results of such an assessment and 'find himself' in the description. Everyone can benefit from the self-knowledge and knowledge of others that it provides.

If you think that I am presenting a tool, a technology, that is marginal—you are wrong! In the near-century since it was formalized, probably <u>50 million people</u> worldwide have used it in their workplaces, in their schools, in their families. Millions more have used it informally to understand what makes them tick a bit more clearly. It is used by so many because of its simplicity and its successes in guiding us to make improvements in our interactions with all the people in our world: there is less misunderstanding and more understanding; there is less resistance and more harmony; there is less gossip and complaining and more true communication and sharing; there is less conflict and more co-operation.

In the workplace, it is used to place people more suitably in jobs in relation to their behavior styles alongside their skill set. It is used to develop communication effectiveness amongst people on teams, and between management and employees. When it is used to do so, smoother and more efficient teamwork is facilitated, and people are happier in their work, because they feel heard and valued for their uniqueness. When people are happier in their work, they do it better and often more quickly, and stay in jobs longer.

Families use them for similarly obvious reasons. Husband and wife come to understand each other's communication style and expectations more readily, and learn how tiny shifts in or adaptations of their own patterns can create a more harmonious interaction together. Parents and children can open up the lines of communication where they might have been closed down. Every family member feels valued, heard, understood.

More and more often today, guidance counselors in schools, career counselors in universities, as well as family counselors helping adults and children get through hard times often use similar personality or behavioral assessment tools.

You might say that four styles cannot possibly be enough to describe every person on the planet. I would like to make it clear that we are, each of us, multilayered, multifaceted individuals who indeed display an identifiable and very complete set of personality traits. Someone might describe himself as 'a simple man with simple tastes', but none of us are 'just one thing'. Note that this book is not the assessment. Nonetheless, you can use this book without completing a formal assessment, and gain deep knowledge into other people's styles and what makes them tick. You can use this book to understand yourself better. You can use this knowledge to better appreciate the results of a full **DISC** profile, should you (or your family members or work teams) ever decide to sit for one.

I say this as my disclaimer, but also to encourage you to continue reading all the remaining chapters to discover who you are, how you are—and as your gateway to discovering who and how other individuals you frequently interact with are. Although using just the four **DISC** behavior styles is simple, it can allow you to learn a lot about the family of man.

Such an assessment reveals to you your *typical* way of approaching any work or job you do—your *usual* behaviors in normal circumstances as you deal with life's tasks and the people in it. It also reveals how you are likely to behave in *stressful* circumstances—this is what I call '*extreme*' or '*ratcheted up*' behaviors in later pages.

In four separate chapters, I present the complete list of behaviors, attitudes, perspectives, needs, fears, motivations and behaviors of one of the **DISC** styles. But first, let's get a slighter broader framework.

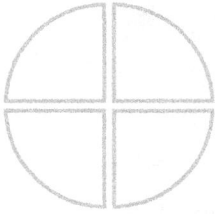

A Simple DISC Profiling

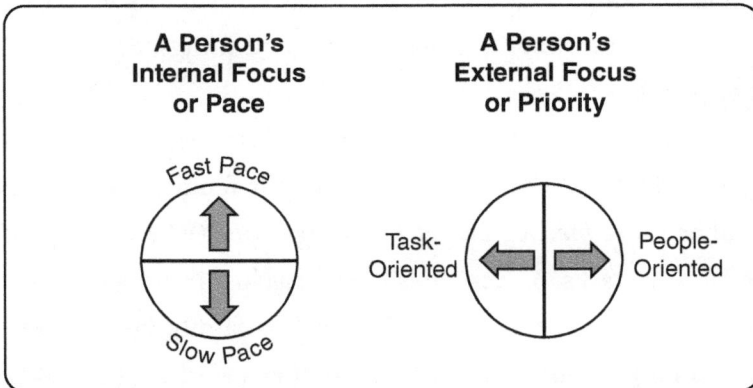

A Person's Internal Focus or Pace	A Person's External Focus or Priority
Fast Pace / Slow Pace	Task-Oriented ← → People-Oriented

Two Fundamental Observations

THIS DISC profile or assessment that I am discussing gets its start with 2 fundamental observations about humans. Let's call them two aspects of human behavior you can readily see by watching anyone at work or at play.

In the preceding chapter, I gave you a sneak peek of one of them. **DISC** looks at your preferred behaviors regarding 'people versus things' (or tasks, as I prefer to call it). Do you remember your response? Are you someone who is more at ease with tasks or with people? Let's examine that some more, since it is so basic to our study of behavior.

What is Your External Focus?

A basic observation anyone can make about an individual is what they focus on 'out in the world.' What external focus do they show? It will be either a focus on tasks and things, or a focus on other people.

Humans are usually either more task-oriented or more people-oriented. Look at someone in your family. Is this family member, ***more focused on getting things done*** (where 'things' are the same as 'tasks' or 'activities'), perhaps lost in the task until it is done correctly or completed? Or is this family member ***more focused on the people around him***, perhaps working on building relationships with those people, or paying attention to their feelings and desires, or working hard to please others?

In the first case, you are looking at a _task-oriented_ individual. In the second case, you are looking at an individual who is more _people-oriented_.

Yes, some individuals find it very easy to move from one focus to the other, as circumstances require. Yet there are individuals who seem stuck in one or the other. Is one good and the other bad? Not at all! It is just who they are!

Start today observing the people around you for Task versus People Orientation. Notice who seems to externally focus only on people—and avoids getting started on tasks, projects or work to be done. Notice who seems to focus much more (or with greater comfort) on external tasks, activities, and things to get done—but might shy away from interaction with others. Just notice. How does your own preference fit in? What about your family members or your boss?

What is Your Internal Focus?

As for the second aspect, we might call it your 'personal pace,' your internal driver or motor. In general, we say a pace is fast or slow. We'll tell a friend to slow down or hurry up.

You can also watch people in their day-to-day life and notice how they tend to be one or the other of these two paces to some greater or lesser degree.

Have you noticed how some people seem revved up and ready to go really quickly? They roll out of bed and are ready to start their day with enthusiasm. They are gregarious, and *jump into their day really quickly*. In other words, they engage their internal motor quickly, and move into a high gear right away. We call these individuals *'fast-paced.' They seem outgoing.* Some are so fast-paced they are like a whirlwind. Others just move and walk and talk so fast that you really need to 'hold on' to keep up with them.

On the other hand, we can observe individuals who are slower to engage or turn the key in the ignition of their motor. They seem to have their internal motors set at a slower 'rate per minute.' They are a bit more reserved and cautious about jumping in. In other words, they hang back, move at a more moderate, or even slower pace—and this is visible to any observer. We call these individuals *'slow-paced.' They seem reserved.* They walk and talk slowly, in a measured way. Some of the slower-paced people might lead you to prod and tell them to 'spit it out' when they talk or to 'hurry it up' when they are doing a task or walking slower than you'd like.

Now look at the chart at the beginning of this chapter. Where do you fit in? What about those family members you were observing, or your boss?

Putting It Together

If you are good at math, you know that if we have two traits in each category, we can easily come up with four combinations describing the individuals around us:

- → Fast-moving and Task-oriented
- → Fast-moving and People-oriented
- → Moderate- to slow-moving and People-oriented
- → Moderate- to slow-moving and Task-oriented

Your job, before moving into the next chapter, is to look at yourself and the people around you whom you believe you know the best, and see how you and they fit in the above pairings! Do that now. I'll have some charts for you after we have looked at the four **DISC** styles that pull these aspects of behavior into all four of the **DISC** styles, too.

Examples of the Orientation Pairs:

Leila is outgoing (her internal focus) and task-oriented (her external focus). You notice that her gestures and her walking pace tend to be quick. She is quite happy to chat with people, is quite cheerful and friendly to everyone. She's the one moving quickly from group to group at events, making sure she meets and speaks with everyone. But you also notice something else about Leila: When she has been given a task (or set one for herself), she can focus on it with such fierce concentration that you could put a loud orchestra in the room and she would not be distracted from the task at hand.

Laleen is outgoing (her internal focus) and people-oriented (her external focus). Like Leila, she keeps a pretty fast pace and is gregarious and talkative in her fast, cheery way. Because Laleen is both outgoing *and* people-focused, she is also great at developing relationships. She is the one you go to with your question, "Do you know anyone who _____?" because she knows so

many people and has such good rapport with them—
and is happy to bring you together. Nothing would
please her more than to create a great new relationship
between people she has introduced!

Kelvin is reserved (his internal focus) and people-oriented (his external focus). Kelvin is visibly reserved—
it's in his body language. He never, ever moves fast—
not eating, not dressing, not working, not talking. He
drives his family crazy at meals, because they have long
since finished and cleaned up—and he is still sitting
there, contentedly eating. Everyone can also easily see
that he is focused, though, on other people's feelings
and desires. He'll formulate his sentences and comments for people's approval. He'd never intentionally
hurt anyone's feelings with his deeds or words, and is
always trying to give them what they want to hear (in
his opinion). People call on Kelvin for his dual qualities of quiet reserve and people-focus when they need
dispute resolution: He is quite diplomatic and listens
carefully to all parties in any disagreement.

Kahlil is reserved (his internal focus) and task-oriented (his external focus). Everyone can see that he
is a measured and moderately-paced person in word
and action. He is also noticeably quiet, not usually
participating in conversation unless asked specific
questions (and then he is brief and to the point—and

goes back into his corner). He would rather go into his workspace and work alone on the project he is assigned than 'mess around' in a group. His combination of reserve and task-orientation lead him to only show his work results when he is personally satisfied that he has done things not only by the book, but completely and accurately.

Jumping Right in with a Simple DISC Assessment

I know you are getting more and more impatient with all this theory and want to jump right in and find out how you are positioned. Let's now do a simple **DISC** assessment, and then in the next chapters we will dive into the details of what the **D, I, S,** and **C** each mean.

I told you that **DISC** assessments were just about choosing your preferred answers to a series of questions. In this 'simple DISC,' however, it is even easier: You are just assigning numbers to words.

In the chart below, move *horizontally* and rank the four words in that **row** from 1 to 4. Assign a **1** to the word that is the **least like you**. Assign a **4** to the word that is the **most like you**. Then use a 2 and a 3 for the other words in that row, with **2 being somewhat unlike you**, and **3 being somewhat like you**. You will use the numbers 1, 2, 3 and 4 <u>one time each per row</u> in that way.

Thus, in the top line where I give an example, I've marked 1 for argumentative—it is very unlike me! I mark 4 for fun-loving—this word is the most like me among the four words given on the row. 'Logical' qualifies as 'somewhat unlike me,' so I assign 2. 'Patient' qualifies as 'somewhat like me,' so I give that word a 3. Then, I move to the next line and do the same for all the rows of words.

You assign a number that represents your ***personal preferences right now***, not what you think might be best (and certainly not what you think others would like you to be).

When done, add the vertical columns up, and put the number next to Total.

The Simple DISC Assessment

1	Blunt	4	Fun-Loving	3	Patient	2	Logical
	Assertive		Expressive		Agreeable		Accurate
	Blunt		Extroverted		Cooperative		Cautious
	Competitive		Fun-Loving		Kind		Conscientious
	Daring		Impulsive		Listener		Factual
	Demanding		Lively		Patient		Formal
	Direct		Optimistic		Peaceful		Logical
	Forceful		Sociable		Security		Obedient
	Risk Taker		Spontaneous		Stable		Organized
	Strong-Willed		Talkative		Supportive		Perfectionist
	Take Charge		Trusting		Warm-hearted		Reserved
	Total		**Total**		**Total**		**Total**

When you add up the four totals you should get 100. If not, check your math! Now write the letter **D** above the first (left-hand) column, **I** above the second column from the left, **S** above the third column from the left and **C** above the last (right-hand) column.

Put each of your scores here again, under the **DISC** names:

D-Dominance	I-Influence	S-Steadiness	C-Conscientious

Circle your scores in each column of the chart on the next page. Note if any scores are above 30. Do you have one score **significantly higher** than the other three? That is what I will be calling in the next four chapters a '**strong style**,' and you'll want to read all about it. It's not good. It's not bad. It is just who you are!

Do you have two scores that are **equal** to each other, and higher than the other two on the chart? You will be interested, in that case, to read the chapters about both of these behavioral styles, too. Are you seeing how you have a blend of styles? It is not better or worse than having one strong style—it is just *your* style!

Are all your scores about the same within 2 to 4 points? Keep reading, because (just as in the above two cases), you will want to understand all four of the **DISC** styles to recognize and position yourself.

	D-Dominance	I-Influence	S-Steadiness	C-Conscientious
Extreme HIGH	40	40	40	40
	38	38	38	38
	36	36	36	36
	34	34	34	34
	32	32	32	32
	30	30	30	30
	28	28	28	28
Midline	26	26	26	26
	24	24	24	24
	22	22	22	22
	20	20	20	20
	18	18	18	18
	16	16	16	16
	14	14	14	14
	12	12	12	12
Extreme LOW	10	10	10	10

In any of these cases, there is no reason to applaud and no reason to despair! In the **DISC** assessment there is absolutely nothing judgmental. The **DISC** assessment is simply a start to helping you understand your behavioral traits, your motivations, and how you act or react when faced with people and faced with tasks to perform.

Here is a quick taste of what your scores might mean. It is not meant to be complete—not yet! With a simple **DISC** assessment such as this, my goal is only to give you a taste of this profile or assessment and what you can learn from it if you do the full **DISC** profile at any time. More details can be found on each style in the next four chapters, so read on to discover yourself!

	D-Dominance	I-Influence	S-Steadiness	C-Conscientious
The Quiz Measures:	How you solve problems and react or act when faced with challenges.	How you attempt to influence or persuade other people.	The pace at which you undertake activities and responsibilities.	How you respond to rules and regulations set by other people for you or your team.
The Higher Scores Mean:	You are more active and aggressive when attempting to overcome problems and obstacles. You are quicker to anger than others.	You are more verbal and persuasive when attempting to influence another person's or group's perspective. You are more joyful and optimistic than others.	You prefer to start & complete one project at a time. You are also more reluctant to embrace change. You are less emotional & more difficult to read than others.	You more readily comply to rules, guidelines or mandates set or imposed by others. You are more motivated out of fear than other emotions.
The Lower Scores Mean:	You have a greater tendency to collect information before making a decision. You are slower to anger.	You use data and facts more readily. You are more pessimistic.	You want a faster pace and change. You are more emotional and expressive.	You challenge rules and seek independence. You are more fearless than other people.

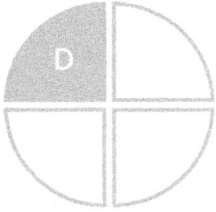

Chapter 5

Position Yourself in the Bigger Pattern: The 'D'

REMEMBER WHAT DISC stands for? Each of the letters stands for the name of the behavioral category. **D** is for *dominance*, but keep in mind that this word is just a memory jogger for this rich, multi-faceted pattern of behavior.

Keep in mind that although you may find yourself strongly in this **D** category, not all the qualities, descriptions and behaviors included in the **D** category will apply to you.

Likewise, no matter how strongly you are situated in this category, you need to look for traits you also possess from the other three categories of behavior—so keep on reading the following chapters, too. In other words, make no assumptions and read all four chapters to see how you may fit into any . . . or all . . . of them.

A Word of Caution

I will be describing each behavior style as if a single person could be only a **D,** with no consideration for the other styles—a 'pure' **D,** or a 'strong' **I,** etc. However, please keep in mind that . . .

Virtually no one is only one single style and nothing else!

That means that my descriptions in each chapter of the four styles may seem a bit heavy or 'over the top' sometimes. Simply view them as an enormous basket of options that a 'strong' **D** or 'strong' **I, S or C** individual is given and can choose from to create the unique individual he or she really is. In being so complete in my descriptions, my goal is to give you all you need to fully understand and identify the patterns that each style holds.

Where Are These D People?

Rest assured, we need all four behavior types in people to make the world go 'round, and to make things interesting!

There are different opinions even among experts about what proportion of each of these styles exist in any population. Some say it is about equally divided, but one researcher's survey determined that **D** people are only about 10% of any population (see the **Resources** section for the work of Robert A. Rohm, PhD). I am going to use his numbers, but keep in mind that there is still debate about them. As you read, you will know exactly where to find 'all of these people.' Recognizing them will be a fun exercise!

If some of the **D** descriptions you will be discovering in the next pages worry you, and you wonder how to get along with those **D** people—relax! If you are a bit anxious about the need to change your own **D** aspects to be more 'likable' or to 'fit in' better—relax! We will discuss all of this and more in the coming pages and chapters. It will be easier than you think to understand all the styles, including your own. It will be easier than you think to learn how to use this new knowledge to get along better with all kinds of people.

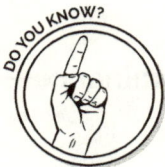

The 'D'—Do You Know Anyone Like This?

As you read the stories of any people I present to you, do two things. First, see if you recognize yourself in any of the descriptions I give about the person's behavior style. Second, see if anyone you know (or know of, like a celebrity or public figure) comes to mind as someone displaying these behaviors. Just like the 'ordinary' people we interact with every day, public personalities are an open book for us to read, too—when we know what to watch for.

Jim is a dynamic, get-it-done kind of person. He has always held high-level management positions in quite large and complex organizations, and is currently the director in charge of security at a corporation employing 8,000 people. He gets impatient (and has been known to even doze off, so fortunately he is the boss!) in long, drawn-out meetings at work, where his peers and subordinates just seem to *talk* about getting things done or endlessly review potential solutions to problems, rather than actually going out and *doing* them once and for all. Long conversations and inactivity are not his style. Just like his meetings at work, even with those he loves he is not verbose. In his leisure time at home, he always seems to have long to-do lists of things that need repairing or improving—and he loves doing it all himself and knowing it is done, rather than hiring someone else to do it.

Memory Jogging Words for Dominance— Is This You?

Remember the **DISC** descriptive word for the **D** style is **dominance.** But like the other behavioral styles, **D** is much more than this single thing!

This said, I would like to use other **D**-behavior words beginning in the letter **D** to help you remember and also understand the individuals around you who may be deploying these **D** behaviors.

A **D** person is also a:

Doer, driver *and* **director, dynamo**

"Done" is a key word for the **D.** You're good at getting tasks done and done well. Do you know anyone whose motto seems to be "Let's just get it *done*"? That is a doer—a **D** person.

A **D** individual is:

Dynamic, *quickly* **decisive, determined, dogmatic, domineering** *and . . . sometimes seems* **dictatorial, dramatic, demanding** *or* **defiant** *of outside authority*

. . . .
QUICK QUIZ: Can you go back into the story of Jim, on the previous page, and underscore the descriptive words and phrases that show how he is behaving from a purely **D** style?
. . . .

When it comes to making a quick judgment call on the behavior pattern of an individual, there are two quick ways to find out what his or her strongest behavior style might be.

Keep Up with the D

One indication of a person's behavior style is about *speed*. "Dynamo" comes to mind for the true **D**. A fast pace suits the **D** perfectly. So does any task that lets the **D** be his own natural fast-and-furious self-starter.

Do you know anyone who often says things like, "Chop, chop! Let's get moving! Hurry it along, folks! Just do it." Do you know anyone who is always moving, doing, active—sort of revved up like a high-speed sports car? **D**'s like things fast-paced! That is the 'dynamo' aspect of the dynamic, driven **D** person.

I mentioned that **D**'s like things to move quickly—at a fast pace. Connected to this affinity for speed, the **D** may very well be your 'early adopter' when it comes to newest, fastest, most performing technologies and devices or equipment. If it is new and fast—our friend, the **D,** will want to be first to have it, test it and show it off.

This 'need for speed' may tire others out as they watch a **D** at work or play, but that is just how they are! And it is a simple way to recognize the **D**.

Are D's Thing or People Oriented?

The second big clue that you might be looking at a **D** is by observing his or her *preference for tasks*. A true **D**, when given a choice to interact and deal with people or to interact and deal with tasks, will choose the task orientation every time.

If you are looking at a strong **D** style, that **D** will display a definite task orientation—a comfort and delight in dealing with tasks, processes and things to get done.

A 'task orientation' is the **D's** preference (and indeed, skill) to interact with an event or circumstance, rather than people. You prefer to 'get into the nuts and bolts of things—and *now!*' What is more, you are likely to walk off all alone to complete or deal with that task. The **D** is not really the best choice when a good 'people-person' is needed!

If something at home or at work is not getting done, and you are in ultimately in charge, what can you do? Go to a busy **D**, and *challenge* him or her to get it done and get it done right . . . but be prepared for some occasional low-quality results (and a need for the **D** to go back to the drawing board) due to rushing the job! A **D** is so task-oriented that throwing down a challenge to complete one is right down his alley—especially when you say, "We need it *right away*" or "and I don't care how you get it done!" That speaks directly to a **D's** face-paced personality and his inner need to do things his way!

Back to Jim, our strong **D** manager from the beginning of this chapter . . .

With such a large number of employees and a business location right in the heart of the big city, parking and other types of transit options for staff had always been an issue for the corporation's leadership. Jim has specifically been tasked (notice the word 'tasked' here is so highly appropriate for his behavior style) with choosing and implementing a solution to create 1,500 additional parking spaces, with no new land to create them on. Committees have met, over and over again, and discussed a great number of potential solutions—but much to Jim's past chagrin never came to an agreed solution for implementation. Now the ball is in his court, and he is the one individual among 8,000 who has been authorized to decide! He loves it!

Needless to say, Jim already has a particular action plan in mind. All he needs to do is write it up, put it on the record by sending it to the executive committee, hire one of the construction companies that he has shortlisted—and *get going*! He is quite excited about finally seeing a solution implemented. And (this is a great aspect of the project in his mind) he doesn't have to report in to huge committees about progress—he is in sole charge.

Smart people on the executive committee had very likely observed not only Jim's personal skill set and capabilities, and his sound perspective on this specific matter, but observed that he was a strong task-oriented, results-focused, take-charge-of-things **D,** and would get the parking solution completed that was right for the company. And indeed, he did!

Some canny observer was probably thinking of a pure **D** when he coined the maxim, *"If you want something done, ask a busy person to do it."*

It's not the people who will be your primary concern in any crisis that may arise, but how to deal with the tasks of resolving it. If you are a strong **D** style, you will agree that you are quite comfortable with tasks! But does this mean you are 'no good' with people? No, not necessarily! Please keep reading the remaining **DISC** chapters to get more insight into this aspect of your own behaviors.

You Might Be a D If . . .

As promised, not all behaviors of this style are described by words beginning in **D**! This was just a way to jog your memory about this style later when you are looking at yourself and others.

As we dive even deeper into the **D** patterns of behavior, please keep in mind that I am describing the nonexistent *'pure'* **D** behavior style. Everything I say about this, and each other individual style, must therefore be taken with the proverbial grain of salt. You will see why when I discuss combinations of the **DISC**, or 'blended styles.'

For now, however, let's continue studying further signs that help you to determine if you, or someone you know, might be a strong **D**. To start, I'll just tell you about a strong **D** individual, in no particular order of importance, and then I'll break it down for you in the next sections.

A Snapshot of the D Style

D's fear loss of control over things which might keep them from empowering others to act. It is important for **D's** to meet their goals and they feel exhilarated when they have achieved them. They always set challenging goals—sometimes others look at the goal and say, "No way can he do that," but the **D** is a believer! They really hate it (and things can get nasty) when someone tries to take advantage of them—so don't do it! **

** A word about using all of the information
I am presenting in these pages:

Learning about others' typical behaviors and motivations and such is not a 'license' to use the information to take undue advantage of another person. If you 'know' how an individual gets 'stirred up,' or what he 'just hates,' or what she views as 'real punishment,' do not use that information against the individual as any kind of leverage! All people are capable of seeing your ploy! Knowing these patterns gives you numerous beneficial and mutually-accepted ways of getting along, getting someone to do something, or getting them to work better in groups, etc. Use this new information to move people into and keep them in a *comfort zone*, for best results and interactions. Be wise about how you use knowledge like this (and we can say the same about all types of knowledge . . .)

D's like to get things done quickly—or to believe that they can. This means that they grow impatient if things take longer than planned. **D's** grow impatient if things don't go as smoothly as they think they should. **D's** go for taking action, getting immediate results, making decisions quickly, solving problems with no fuss.

D's like to have control over their work environment and other people's activities in it. They appreciate being given responsibility for results and the freedom to achieve them their way. **D's** like to be given opportunities for advancement in the workplace and in their personal life.

D's hate being questioned about or micromanaged in any task. **D's** really, really don't like to be told what specific steps to take or how to do any task. They stay away from routine or predictability.

That's it for my quick snapshot. To explain things in more detail, and to expand the description of this behavior style, let's look at verbal and non-verbal communication, what motivates the **D**, and what type of career path is most suitable for such a behavior style as this **Dominant D.**

Key Spoken Words and Phrases of the D Style

"Challenge" is a key word to stimulate and get action from all strong **D's.** They thrive on challenges! All you need to tell them is <u>what</u> the end-goal is—but definitely *not* <u>how</u> to reach it—and the **D** is ready to go!

Hearing, "This might be a challenge for you, Miss **D**," gets a **D** very, very excited, and she is then likely to respond with something like:

- "I'm on that job!", "I'm on it!"

- "Let's decide (resolve) these two little issues quickly, and I'll get the project going."

- "I'll have it done before you know it."

- "Let's start right now."

- "It involves some change / some risk, and that's good for us, because . . . "

Do you know the Nike sport shoe company? My guess is that the advertising person or the Nike manager who thought up their famous motto "Just Do It" was probably a **D** individual! The **D's** motto might be "Go for it!" as well as "Just do it."

If the **D** is not feeling challenged, he may outright dare his boss by saying, "Challenge me! I can do it!"

As an extension of that mindset, the **D** acts and speaks as though his philosophy is, "I want this yesterday!" because the **D** tends to be quite impatient. He is impatient with too much talk, others' procrastination, and project start-dates that are set too far in the future.

Regarding rules, and particularly social rules, the **D** is the most likely of all four behavior styles to either break the rules or simply disregard them.

When the **D** speaks on any subject or gives direction to someone, it is with no fluff. He cuts to the bottom line and addresses the heart of the matter right away. No dancing around the matter at hand for him! He's brief and may assume you know the details and steps involved (because he won't think to bring them up) and probably even speaks a bit formally or dogmatically. He often sounds directive (not to mention dictatorial or pushy) about things. A **D** may come to you, with 'recommendations' he prefaces with firm 'orders,' such as, "You have to [do this or that];" You must [do it like this, do it by that time];" "You really should . . . "

As a matter of voice style, a **D** is very likely to speak loudly or firmly and decisively. **D's** speak bluntly (though not unkindly), and typically are quite concise. **D's** are frustrated by people who do not understand immediately, who need detailed **instruction**, or who are unwilling to follow the directive (or make a change). This said, don't despair: If you need more details from the **D**, you're going to have to ask for them with clear, pointed questions. Be prepared to quickly note his brief, pointed answer!

Though he or she often means well, the **D** interrupts frequently—especially interrupting slow talkers, or people who like to 'hear themselves speak,' and other types of verbose time-wasters. When the **D** doesn't 'mean well'? He uses verbal interruptions to take over territory or to take back control of a situation. As you now know, the **D** is very controlling!

Key Body Language of the D Style

We all use body language as a key aspect of our interpersonal communication. Combined with our **DISC** behavior patterns, they make us uniquely who we are. Luckily for us, each of these four behaviors also uses some specific and discernible body language. What about the **D**?

Looking at the body language of a **D** when speaking to others, he is not unkind or dismissive of others. Quite the contrary, he boldly looks others in the eye and has steady eye contact. The **D** shakes hands firmly and will typically have the first word as a signal of dominance, spoken in an assertive, confident voice.

He just may (unconsciously, as with most of these behaviors we are discussing) appear to make his body appear taller or bigger, occupying more space—in other words, more dominant, in relation to or in the perception of those with him in that space. This works for the territorial **D** and gives him a sense of ownership and authority over the physical space . . . and the people in it. The strong **D** is more than happy to sit at the head of a table, step onto a podium, or to stand at the lectern—this, too, gives him the feeling of territorial control and authority he desires.

Do the **D's** you know smile a lot? Maybe not. This never means that person is unhappy or displeased! A still face, impassive and unexpressive, is a **D** trademark.

Remember that a **D** is a doer, a fast-moving, active individual—very, very rarely content to just sit around and wait for something to happen. Because of that, the **D** will act physically restless and impatient if things seem to slow down around him. He's the one that gets people and projects moving along—at his faster pace. When it is time to start the new project or go somewhere, the **D** quite literally jumps into action and is off and running.

Knowing a bit now about the **D** individuals' behavior style, how do we help each other thrive and live our fullest potential? If you are a parent, think of your strong **D** child. If you are supervisor of a strong **D** employee, how do you see this employee portrayed in this next set of descriptions? If it is you who are the strong **D**, have you felt that these **D** attributes are beneficial or detrimental to your interactions with people in your personal life, to your current career path, to your relationships at work? Just keep your responses in mind, because as you read, you will learn a bit more about what to do about them.

Demotivating, Discouraging and Distressing the D

You might get some cues from a **D's** body postures or positions when he is less than motivated, less than enthusiastic—even outright distressed or angry. Why? Like all people, the **D** will not be happy, nor will he thrive in some specific types of situations or under some conditions (most of which should start to be predictable to you!) that rub his natural style the wrong way. Sometimes it is not real unhappiness or even frustration. It is just an inability to perform optimally and operate within his personal comfort zone. Here are some types of circumstances that can specifically distress the **D.**

What I call demotivating circumstances are those that rub contrary to a person's behavior style. Sometimes it is done purposefully or strategically, but most of the time, we all just want to get along. So, take note!

Do any of the following, and you'll be demotivating, discouraging or even angering the **D**:

→ Show him up as a weakling or a 'softie'

→ Challenge him in how he has done things or is planning on doing something

→ Tell him how to do things, how he needs to approach a project, circumstance or individual

→ Tell him he's going to be under tight supervision or that he has to 'report in' frequently to a person of higher authority

→ Deny him the responsibility or leadership for a project or task, or deny him full access to the resources and people he needs to perform

→ Require him to sit at a desk doing repetitive, routine work until further notice

→ Slow him down in any number of ways

Watch for this **D's** reactivity when any of these circumstances are activated! The D will react negatively or with some kind of protest in any of these cases because the **D**—as you can now easily guess—needs to write his own rules and to determine his own way of doing things! At best, he'll circumvent the 'new rules' and find a workaround. At worst, he'll explode in anger and make life very, very uncomfortable for those around him.

What Motivates or Stimulates the D?

The **D** is obviously motivated by things he likes and demotivated by what he does not—just like every other individual we are describing in these pages. That's human nature!

However, patterns help us once again to see what motivates or excites the strong **D** individual, so that (in the best of cases and when at all possible) we can give the **D** more of what makes him effective . . . and happy.

Here is what motivates the strong **D**:

→ **Action**—being called on or allowed to take immediate action to achieve an agreed result.

→ **Challenge; new opportunities**—throwing down a seemingly impossible challenge is a surefire way to get the **D** excited and moving into action. A **D** simply cannot resist a challenge!

→ **Calculated risk**—the **D** is always confident that it will pay off.

→ **Goals**—the **D's** love to set and get their goals, so help them set large ones and small ones. A **D** is very goal-oriented.

→ **Ambition and competition, winning**—pit the **D** against another team or company, or set out an award or reward for winning. The **D** will eat out of your hand, and probably be the winner.

→ **Control; doing it his way; freedom**—the **D** will always be an accountable and responsible person, but give him independence, a degree of power and authority over the task at hand to motivate the **D** at the highest level. He will take charge and do things his way, and rest assured—it will be done well and quickly with minimal fuss and muss.

Those are some of the approaches to keeping the **D** happily involved and productive from start to finish!

You have surely noticed that the motivators are the opposites of the demotivators. Of course! And it will be so for all the other behavior styles.

Creating such a motivating environment for the strong **D** is a great way to keep him happy and productive. Remember that the **D** loves the opportunity to show that he is the best, that he can take responsibility, that he can perform important tasks or take charge in a leadership role. He naturally loves to do things his way. If you have the ways and means to create such an environment for your strong **D**—be it at home or in the workplace—he or she will do great things . . . and you have a great ally on your team who appreciates that you have 'let him loose' to 'be the best he can be.'

Remember my description of Jim at the beginning of the chapter.

Jim's superiors on the executive committee entrusted him with a task-oriented project that was in the interest of the entire company to have done correctly. They did this knowing his **D** behavior style as well as his past record of performance. They essentially gave him a budget, a deadline and set him loose. Ah, the **D** loves that and always rises to the challenge!

Jim is thriving primarily though in his management position overseeing *matters of security*. In his corporation, security is about 'things or tasks to perform'—as an example, controlling access to the entire site that is manned by his teams of security guards, equipping all verified employees and guests with digitized identification cards, digital access points on buildings and doorways so that the activities of those areas remain secure from unauthorized individuals, and so on.

Yes, Jim has quite a few people under his supervision as well. But all his people also work with 'things to do or tasks to perform.' So, when we see that Jim has a strong **D** behavior style, he is working in a perfect task-oriented career.

Talents and Careers of the D

It has been shown time and time again to be true that typical **D's** share certain talents with each other. It harkens back to the phenomenon called 'patterns.' In other words, we can say that the following types of strengths, traits, qualities or characteristics are common among **D's**, and lead them naturally to certain career paths.

Whether you are an observant parent, a friend, a co-worker or a business supervisor of the **D**, you will certainly see one or many of these characteristics in your **D**. To know them is to use them or adapt to them for greatest success and harmony! As you read, think about jobs, professions and career paths that call for such qualities.

A **D** typically exhibits:

→ a dictatorial or bossy style of leadership
→ a strong will to achieve and do
→ comfort in fast-paced environments; fast work performance
→ competitiveness
→ confidence, self-confidence
→ decisiveness
→ direct, to-the-point communication
→ drive for immediate action
→ drive to achieve goals set by himself or others

→ focused determination

→ independence and assertiveness

→ initiative

→ task orientation

→ time efficiency

Let's see more about the strong **D**'s best career paths, since, as you guess, Jim's type of work would not be available to everyone, **D** or not! If you are the **D** we are discussing, you very likely already know if you are in your most suitable career or not. If you are, you feel comfortable, effective, productive, and appreciated! If you need guidance in the matter of career choice, keep reading!

What kinds of careers are potentially great matches for strong **D** individuals? It absolutely depends on individual skills and talents, and often on the type of education a person has received.

Consider some of these careers for the **D**:

→ Business owner

→ Coach to sports groups or athletes, coach or consultant to businesses

→ Company leadership positions: chairman, chief executive or president, directors, department head, managers and supervisors, factory foreman, leaders of product lines, project managers or negotiation leadership

→ Leader of creative groups, in roles like producer, director or musical conductor

→ Military officer, at best in charge of 'things' rather than personnel

→ Pilot

→ Policeman or security guard

→ Political leaders

→ Restaurant maître d', hotel concierge

→ Teachers in charge of their own classrooms

Remember what I have been saying about 'strong' **D's**. This whole chapter (as will be the chapters on **I**, **S**, and **C** individuals) makes an assumption that there is a 'pure **D**' out there somewhere. As I have said, that is simply not true! **D** is a strong aspect of the individuals I have been describing, but far from their only aspect. Because of this, some strong **D** individuals may find that the careers I have listed hold no interest or potential for them whatsoever. But keep on reading, because those of you in that position will certainly see that you have at least one other strong behavior style and two or three weaker ones which will temper your overall **D** behaviors and lead you to other more appropriate career choices.

Do's and Don'ts for D's

We are looking at four different patterns of behavior in this book, which means that anyone who is not your own behavior style will probably behave in ways that you don't expect.

Can we do anything to 'help' other individuals get along with us better? Yes! Here are a few things you can definitely do to help the **D** feel more comfortable with you while still feeling that he or she has some control, followed by a few things that you certainly don't want to do to a **D** if your objective is to keep the peace, allow productivity or just get along. Lastly, do whatever you reasonably can to show the **D** that he/she has the controls—they thrive on being in charge and driving the action.

Do This

When speaking to a **D**, think 'bullet points.' This will help you be brief, direct and to the point—which is what a **D** appreciates in communication with other people. In speaking with the **D**, keep your focus solution-oriented, on the business at hand, and about achieving results or a goal. Acknowledge and respect the **D**'s authority and initiative, perhaps using phrases like, "Sure, you're in charge," "You're the boss," "You're the decision-maker." If a **D** sets a deadline for you—keep it! If a **D** is your boss—stay productively busy, because a **D** can detect busywork or idleness a mile away.

Don't Do This

When interacting or collaborating with a **D**, keep your emotions and feelings under wraps—don't express them openly. For those of you who tend to take things personally—don't. It's a waste of time with the **D**, for whom "It's not personal, it's business." If you tend to be a very sociable, humorous or sensitive person—lock it away when you're with a **D**. Don't ramble, repeat yourself, attempt to engage **D's** in any sort of rehashing of a subject, and don't nag them. If you are naturally chatty, forget it when you're with a **D**. That is not the way to get results or action from the **D**! Will a **D** interrupt other people freely? Absolutely. But don't ever try to interrupt a **D** yourself . . .

Key Strengths of the D

Each of the four behavior styles presents significant strengths. The **D** has a commanding presence, lots of drive, lots of energy and a preference for moving at a fast pace, a great deal of self-confidence. As the **D** is strongly task-oriented, he knows how to solve problematical issues and look objectively at them. He has a bold and daring risk taker who likes to take charge—in fact, the **D** makes an excellent leader with a passion for power and decisiveness.

Many of these strengths make the **D** the person we most want to call on for leadership, especially in an emergency situation. A **D** will keep his eye on the ball with focus—which for him is the desired end-result. The **D** leader will tend to give his teams all the tools and various resources they need to achieve his goal his way, which for the **D** is quickly and on schedule, without much discussion.

Weaknesses of the D Behavior Style

Granted, the **D** may not agree that anything I'm going to say in the next lines are actually weaknesses! These weaknesses are, however, perceived by individuals from the other behavior styles.

A **D** is a multitasker. Remember that a **D** is task oriented and enjoys a fast pace, so when we put these two characteristics together multitasking is an obvious **D** trait. Strength or weakness? It's a point of view; this said, if a **D** is simultaneously drafting an email, answering a phone call, signing important documents—we must ask ourselves if the **D** is a superhuman . . . or if mistakes will be made (and often they are). Because of the **D's** preference for fast pace, the **D** will often interrupt a speaker from impatience to get to the point; the **D** is not the best listener. This impatience sometimes also leads to hasty judgments and decision-making, causing a **D** to risk more failures than most people. Because the **D** is not good at expressing his or her own feelings, there is little sympathy for those who are expressive of them.

Are D's Extremes Good or Bad?

You appreciate by now that there are lots of other people out there behaving in ways you may not harmonize with! Some of those individuals respond in the exactly opposite way that you would—or in ways that shock you. Do not be surprised, therefore, when you find that someone who leads with your 'opposite' energy or behavior style tends to see you as negative. For all strong **D's** the strong **S style** is the **DISC** style that is your opposite (more on that later, after you have read all the **DISC** chapters)— and a strong **S** person might see the **D** in a negative light. If not negative per se, others will just have a feeling that they can't easily get along with you or understand your motivations.

As you learn in these pages *why* everyone around you behaves as they do, hopefully your new outlook is that there isn't much that is really negative about people at all—you are just different, and that is neither negative nor positive. It just is!

I have not yet stressed the extremes of the **D** style, as that can be a matter of personal judgment or perspective. However, keep in mind that each style indeed has its particular extremes, which derive from the 'baseline' or 'natural' behaviors—those I have been presenting so far. For any baseline behavior a **D** (and all the other three styles also do this) deploys in normal, everyday circumstances, he or she may have a tendency to 'ratchet it up' or push any of those behaviors into an extreme version of itself in times of stress, pressure or emergency situations. Any style you possess will also ratchet up usual behaviors when you feel you have lost control in some way.

Here is how that might occur in a strong **D** individual. The **D's** usual tendencies shift into their extreme or out-of-control versions, and surge forth as the **D** attempts to gain back control, keep from losing control or to solve and resolve some crisis or emergency.

Are the extremes positive or negative? It would always depend on the circumstances!

D's Extremes

Recklessness, as just one example, is an extreme version of the **D's** innate *bravery*. See if you can identify the **D's** habitual behavior as you read this list of other potential **D** extremes:

→ Challenger to the status quo or authority
→ Workaholic, pushy, fanatical
→ Demanding, dictatorial
→ Bossiness
→ Mercilessness
→ Arrogance
→ Impatience, stubbornness
→ Obsessive
→ Bluntness, rudeness, tactlessness

The D—Is This Someone You Interact with?

Understanding these styles and that everyone has his own combination of them can help you in all your relationships. Adapting (even briefly) to other people's styles—or in the case of a whole team who understands the **DISC** approach, adapting to each other's styles—has many benefits.

Back to Jim, our manager from the beginning of this chapter.

> As a strong **D**, he has realized he has a task-forte, and yet needs to successfully manage other people displaying many behavior combinations different from his own. He knows he needs to increase his people awareness when dealing with his subordinates—at least, he should, if he wants them to perform at their best level of productivity, attention and accuracy. However, the executive who Jim reports to has no real knowledge of behavior styles, so it is also in Jim's best interest, for harmony in the work-place, for him to address his boss's apparent behavior preferences.

What I am describing is Jim's awareness—having studied his own **DISC** report for himself and to enhance his management results—that he must *adapt at least momentarily* to others' behavior styles in order to get them to respond, act and perform optimally and with the greatest degree of comfort and focus. Jim understands that he is not permanently changing his natural behaviors outright, but purposefully modifying his approaches to meet another person's needs and expectations . . . and to get something done with him.

Interacting Successfully with the D

If you have a strong **D** in your work team or at home, how do you interact with him or her? How do you 'manage' all your interactions? Let's look at that now.

The first rule of interacting successfully with any individual whose profile is different from yours is to remember the concept of "expectations."

All of us expect other people to act and react the same way we do. The **D** is no exception. In fact, the **D** may be a little more hard-headed to deal with than the other three profiles! Rest assured, once the **D** individual understands how the other **DISC** profiles operate, he too will, of course, be open to some adaptation.

And that is the second concept to keep in mind—"adaptation." In order to get along with individuals of different behavioral profiles, none of us will have to make dramatic permanent changes in ourselves. We only need to make a momentary adaptation or shift in our natural behaviors in order to come briefly into harmony with the other individual and give others what they need.

Just let the **D** be who he is and how he is. Here is how to shift your natural way of operating to get closer to giving a **D** what he needs:

Keep in mind that an individual responding and reacting from the **D** dimension has one fear above all else—no **D** wants to lose personal control over any situation. Knowing that, you will allow the **D** (as far as it is possible for you, your family or your business organization) to choose how they do any task and how they organize themselves and others to perform any project. You will avoid micromanaging the **D** individual, but come to some agreement in advance on how **D** will let you know that he is or is not making progress or does or does not need your assistance. Stick with facts and get to the point when you speak with the **D**, and write it up briefly if your **D** has a tendency to remember only what he wishes to about your agreement.

Remember that a **D** has a fear of losing control, but on the other side of that equation a **D** is most highly motivated when you throw down a challenge or want the **D** to find a solution to a problem.

Never call the **D** to task in front of other individuals. Do it privately, with confidence, looking your **D** straight in the eye when you tell him or her how he has fallen down on the job. No general complaints about his performance will work with the **D**, so be specific! Assume you were not specific enough about the desired outcome. Remember not to tell a **D** how to achieve the outcome; just make sure the **D** has clearly understood what the goal is.

Keep in mind that the **D** gets impatient and loses focus when there's too much talk. This goes for decision-making. The **D** will tend to rush into a decision and sometimes be wrong. Behind closed doors, point out that the **D** may need to gather more information and strategically project into the future consequences of any decision he makes. Put that responsibility square in his lap as a challenge, and the **D** will perform. Remember that the **D** is solution oriented, results oriented, and task oriented.

In the end, like almost all people, the **D** will welcome all opportunities to get ahead or be rewarded in some way for his successes.

What If I Am Not All This One Style?

Remember that I have encouraged you to go through all 4 **DISC** descriptive chapters first, so that you can get a complete picture of yourself or another individual. Yes, one dimension may be quite strong for you. But as you keep reading, you will discover that you also see yourself in the others! You need to read all four chapters, because virtually no individual is only one behavior style. Like an innovative executive chef, all of us have our own unique 'recipe' of behaviors, motivations, adaptive capability (extremes), strengths and weaknesses (and I have been intentionally repeating that a lot). This first dimension or style—the **strong D**—is no exception, and combines with the three others in some way in almost every case.

In other words, none of us is unidimensional, and thus, even when your **DISC** assessment report shows that you are 'predominantly' or strongly in the **D** dimension, you are not only that— you have some degree and combination of the others within you as well.

So, finish reading about the other three styles, then go to the chapter that illustrates how your behaviors can subtly shift when you add the other dimensions of you to the mix!

Just for Fun

If you are the **D** person I have been describing, or if you have been thinking all along about a person you know who is definitely a strong **D**, have some fun with these shared interests that researchers have discovered among the **D** individuals.

→ Color a **D** gravitates to—Green

→ Animal/pet favored by the **D**—the Doberman Pinscher, whose temperament is fearless and alert, intelligent and confident, energetic and fast-moving (just like a **D**!)

→ Car preferred by **D** drivers—the Mercedes or the Cadillac

→ The **D's** motto in all things—"Just go for it!"

→ Song lyrics that describe the **D** best—"I Did It My Way"

→ The **D's** philosophy—"I want it yesterday!"

→ The **D's** favorite magazine—*Money Magazine*

→ How the **D** treats a target—"Ready . . . Fire . . . Aim!

→ Top two needs experienced by the strong **D**—challenge and dominance

In Summary

Of the four **DISC** styles, the **D** behaviors, motivators and strengths make them the most assertive and forceful of all styles—they want to be in charge, and to charge forward now! If you want to strike fear in the heart of a **D**, take away his personal control over any project or situation—he is willing to take responsibility and be accountable for results, but cannot abide micro-management, being told *how* to go about a task, or that his authority is in question.

Knowing this about a **D,** you'll need to be willing and able to give over all authority to him and get out of his way!

D's thrive on challenges and are not afraid to take a risk when it is the **D** himself who has calculated the risks and rewards of doing so.

Knowing this, you'll prefer putting a confident **D** in charge of any innovation or solution that involves some risk. When the **D** commits, he can and will get it done, even if he has to start over one or more times to get it right.

All **D's** tend to be task-oriented, strong-willed, competitive, results-oriented . . . and self-oriented with a perpetual "What's in it for me?" question on their lips (remember their task orientation; they have little focus other people's opinion or needs).

Knowing this, you won't ask a **D** to be in charge of people-projects, long debates and discussions. You might prefer to simply report to him what the outcome was, and ask him to take it from there.

The strong **D** is fast-moving, loves change, and typically seems energized and energetic. A **D** keeps occupied all day long, with either a string of tasks or with simultaneous projects going on under his purview.

Knowing this, if you are a person or team that needs to take your time for any reason, or have long brainstorming or debate-type discussions, don't ever put a **D** in charge—you will get trampled! And the **D** will become extremely frustrated (or worse) with you and the whole project.

D's communicate with authority and brevity (often mistaking their personal opinions for proven fact), and expect to be understood right away. Long, drawn out discussions are not for them! They tend not to be the best listeners, and when they do listen, we find them interrupting more often than not—they expect everyone to get to the point right away.

Knowing this about a **D,** we need to be somewhat insistent if we need **D's** to hear us out and to consider a point of view that is not theirs.

When presented with a new project, a sticky problem or new challenge, the **D** is thrilled! A **D** hates routine (he finds it tedious and boring) and jumps on the chance to make a change when a challenge is thrown down. **D's** will often ask questions with "What?" such as "What is the bottom line here?" "What results are expected?" Those are always important questions for the **D** who is good at keeping the Big Picture and the ultimate end goal in mind . . . and racing towards it.

Knowing this, don't try to tie the **D** down with report-writing or any kind of ongoing data-rich work for a project. He hates the routine, and you won't be happy with his work.

Non-**D's** see a **D** as impatient with everyone else; they are seen as blunt speakers and leaders (often perceiving the blunt style as rude).

But it is not all bad: Non-**D's** may also admire strong **D's** for their decisiveness, risk tolerance, their get-it-done-now, goal-getting attitude, and their ability to see the Big Picture in an environment of risk and change. This means that they'll call on a strong **D** when they're entering risky territory, need a quick decision for action (often on little information), or a strong person to keep everyone moving resolutely and with focus in the direction of solutions and results.

Are you this **D?** Maybe not! So, read on to discover the 'I', the 'S' and 'C' dimensions.

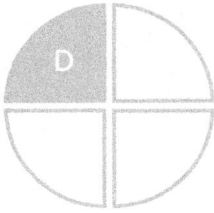

Chapter 5 bis

Charting the D Behavioral Style

TO MAKE referencing the **D** easier for those of you who prefer lists and bullet points, here are the key elements of this ***Dominant*** style below.

D's Top Observable Characteristics

1. Accountable
2. Action-oriented
3. Adventurous
4. Ambitious
5. Competitive
6. Decisive
7. Direct
8. Dynamo
9. Extroverted
10. Fast-paced
11. Forceful and assertive
12. Goal minded
13. Independent
14. Initiative
15. Optimistic
16. Pioneering risk-taker
17. Practical
18. Skeptical
19. Strong-willed, determined and demanding
20. Task-orientation, multi-tasker

D's Typical Body and Verbal Language

D's verbal language:

D's speak:
- Loudly
- Confidently
- Briefly and concisely
- Bluntly (no 'sweeteners' or euphemisms)
- By interrupting—a lot!

D's love to hear these words:
- "This might be a challenge for you."
- "We have a tight deadline."
- "We need you to take the lead on this."
- "Just do it anyway you like; you're on your own."
- D's often say things like:
  - → "I'm on it."
  - → "Let's just get to it now."
  - → "Risk is good for us."
  - → "Let's start now!"

D's body language:

- Look you steadily in the eye
- Make themselves look bigger, taller, more physically dominant
- Exhibit a still, impassive, unexpressive face
- Fast moving and active

D's Top Motivators

D's love to be motivated—just like anyone else! They feel motivated and thrive in any environment where they are provided with:

1. Being known/recognized as a problem solver
2. Being known/recognized as talented
3. Challenging (and even many simultaneous) tasks
4. Competition
5. Critical assignments
6. Deadlines, even tight ones
7. Driving, directing people
8. Evaluation based on results
9. Fast pace: being busy, active and occupied
10. Freedom from control, micromanagement or supervision
11. Hard worker
12. Having authority
13. Important tasks, with any non-routine, new, varied activities
14. Making independent decisions
15. Negotiation opportunities
16. Opportunities for accomplishment and advancement
17. Productivity
18. Project management
19. Responsibility, being in charge of projects/people
20. Winning

D's Top Demotivators

D's, like everyone else, hate to be in environments that demotivate them. They get frustrated and feel stuck as we all would, when people don't act like a **D** wants or expects them to, or when circumstances don't meet the **D's** expectations! These might be situations such as these:

1. Apathy in any group in which the **D** must work
2. Disagreement with the **D** or overruled decisions
3. Diving into details is required
4. Easily giving up
5. Evaluation based on relationships
6. Gathering or meeting with no clear goals
7. Lack of promptness, enthusiasm, energy or vigor by others
8. Lack of challenge
9. Lethargy or carelessness about reputation
10. Micro-management or supervision
11. Passive, hesitant or slow reactions from others
12. Questioning decisions
13. Relaxing or lounging about
14. Rigid rules one is expected to respect, strict order
15. Rote tasks and anything resembling routine
16. Slow paced unfolding of any circumstance
17. Stop-and-Go or Stop-and-Wait pace for any reason
18. Sympathy given to anyone providing poor performance
19. Unproductive
20. Wasting time with stories and irrelevant chatter

D's Top Strengths

1. Achiever
2. Commanding, with a passion for power
3. Confidence
4. Courageous, daring, bold
5. Decisive
6. Drive, energy, dynamic
7. Excellent leader in an emergency situation
8. Explain rationally
9. Fast paced
10. Finds opportunities, loves challenge
11. Independent
12. Initiative
13. Knows how to look at and solve problematic issues objectively
14. Optimistic
15. Persistence
16. Pioneering mindset
17. Stimulated by action
18. Strategic thinker
19. Task oriented
20. Willpower

D's Top Weaknesses

Keep in mind that a strong **D** is not likely to agree with me that these are weaknesses! Observers of the **D**, however, may decide that in some circumstances the following 'qualities' are desirable, and in others most definitely irritating to deal with! All behavior is situational!

1. Avoiding Details
2. Blunt
3. Bossy
4. Controversial
5. Dislikes routine
6. Doing many things at once
7. Domineering
8. Egocentric
9. Hasty
10. Impatient with poor performance
11. Interrogator
12. Interrupting the speaker
13. Irritable
14. Machiavellian
15. Not caring for personal excuses
16. Not expressing feelings
17. Not a good listener
18. Oversteps authority
19. Risk taker
20. Unsympathetic

D's Top Extremes

      D's feel they've lost personal control at times—just like we all do. They move into extremes like everyone else when provoked or when they see a need to 'step up' and lead with a firm hand. Some people will see these extremes simply as 'a **D** gone wild.' Maybe, maybe not. Again, behaviors are situational!

1. Aggressive
2. Approaching things/people from 'my way or the highway,' 'win-lose' mindset
3. Arrogant
4. Belittling and rude, sarcastic and scornful, dismissive
5. Controlling
6. Defensive
7. Demanding, coercive, dictatorial
8. Disrespectful
9. Explosive anger
10. Finger pointing
11. Hostile
12. Impatient, argumentative
13. Impetuous
14. Inconsiderate, tactless, prejudiced, insensitive, intolerant
15. Possessive
16. Risk taking, without much prior planning, calculation or attention to details
17. Sabotager
18. Skeptical
19. Unforgiving
20. Workaholic

Top Things to Do for a D

To gain the trust of **D's**, try to _do_ some of the following

1. Ask "what" not "how" questions
2. Be brief, direct and to the point
3. Be independent, take initiative, have goals
4. Focus on solutions, business at hand and achieving results, stay productively busy
5. Give them a guideline of the task
6. Meet deadlines
7. Recognize their accomplishments, help them to feel important, respect their authority
8. Suggest ways for **D's** to achieve results, be in charge, and solve problems
9. When in agreement, agree with facts and ideas rather than the person
10. When problems exist, discuss them in light of how they will hamper accomplishment

Top Things Not to Do with a D

To avoid conflicts with **D's**, _don't do_ the following types of things:

1. Act sensitive
2. Be funny
3. Be irrational
4. Be too sociable
5. Bother them pointlessly
6. Complain to them
7. Confront them during explosive moments
8. Dismiss or ignore his input
9. Expose your feelings
10. Focus on problems
11. Generalize
12. Interrupt them while speaking
13. Make statements to them without support
14. Make them appear inferior
15. Make yourself look smarter than **D's**
16. Nag them
17. Ramble
18. Repeat yourself
19. Take his directness as a personal affront
20. Waste **D's** time with personal issues

And of course—all of us working with a **D** will avoid telling **D's** they 'must' do anything; use 'should' when you advise the **D**!

D's Fears

- Being taken advantage of
- Feeling vulnerable
- Loss of control
- Work in monotonous environments

Top Tips for a D's Growth

Given any individual's starting point, there is always room for personal and professional growth and improvement. **D's** are no exception. They are just as able to shift their awareness of behavior to create more harmony, have better interactions, and help everyone else to thrive. To stretch **D** individuals and facilitate growth, they can make small shifts.

Put more energy into developing harmonious personal relationships.

Pay attention to other team members' ideas until everyone reaches a consensus. This makes you seem/act less controlling and domineering, friendlier and more approachable. Praise others for their courtesy (for their help or participation, or their useful commentaries, etc.) more consistently—just a brief 'Thanks' can be enough!

Related to this, develop coaching skills to help others, coax them along with questions, and sit still long enough to hear and comment on the answers.

Express your feelings a bit more. It doesn't have to be heart-baring, just a quiet remark about your emotion about a thing every once in a while.

Read/reflect on the task vs people orientations and when a shift from one to the other might be helpful.

On a personal level, invite friends for social gathering and relax; spend time with family and friends; share personal stories with others. In other words, *slow down* and enjoy the company of others. Read/reflect about the power of vulnerability—let people get to know you.

Be more aware of rules and punishments—they also apply to you! Read/reflect on autonomy vs responsibility—you are rarely alone to carry out a decision or to achieve a work goal (so remember to involve others, take into account their opinions and needs). Do risk assessment for critical decisions and weigh the pros and cons of your actions/decisions at work or at home. Why? Others are more risk-averse than you and you can respect that difference by slowing down and listing out *with them* the reasons for or against any action.

Reflect on trust—others are capable of taking control; others are worthy of your trust. By showing patience and support for other team members and slowing down your actions and thoughts, by 'actively' listening more and more—people will come to trust you, too. It is a valuable asset to cultivate.

Reflect on control. It is fine to be a strong Big Picture End Goal person. Details, however, matter—to projects and to other people. Delegate dealing with the details or resolve to focus on them yourself. Take time to explain the 'whys' of your statements and proposals. Talk less in meetings and listen and ask more questions (and sit still and listen to answers).

Phrases to Use That Encourage D's Energy

None of these energizing and encouraging phrases will surprise you now that you know the **D** style:

- "I don't care how you do it, just get it done!"
- "We offer great opportunities for advancement in this company."
- "He'll need you to move fast on this project."
- "I want you to be in charge."
- "This is quite a challenge, so we thought of you for the job."
- "Finish this on time and on target, and there's a bonus in it for you."

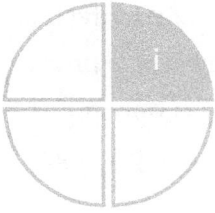

Chapter 6

*Position Yourself
in the Bigger Pattern:
The 'I'*

REMEMBER WHAT DISC stands for? Each of the letters stands for the name of the behavioral category. **D** is for Dominant, and the next one—**I**—is for *Influencer*.

A Word of Caution

Each of us has our own combination of **D, I, S,** and **C** tendencies and patterns, and I will be repeating that often! You will want to resist any tendency to think that any person with strong **I** behaviors, body language, motivations, and so on possesses *only* that single **I** dimension.

In this chapter, I will be describing the *nonexistent* individual who displays a very strong **I** behavior style, and only the elements of this style. No such 'pure **I**' individual exists! It is only for explanatory purposes, and serves to help you understand thoroughly and deeply this behavior style called the **I**.

Where Are These I People?

Researchers disagree, as I have stated in the prior chapter, but individuals with a strong or dominant **I** behavior style represent about 25-35% of the overall population.

There is diversity even in the most homogeneous of families or communities. The world is definitely a more interesting place when people exhibit different backgrounds, beliefs, attitudes and perspectives and opinions. We need all four of these behavior types in people, and they likewise definitely serve to make relationships and interaction interesting! Understanding the four behavior styles will clear up a lot of mysteries that you may have about why people act and react the way they do, and say the things they say.

If you are a parent, understanding these behavior styles might resolve the mystery about why one of your children wants or does not want to follow your prescribed career or education path. It will explain to you why some of your children act gregariously and are outgoing, while one or more of them is shy and retiring. Just keep on reading these chapters about all four behavior styles, and your parenting might just become a bit easier, and hold less mystery—both for you and your children!

If you are an employer, supervisor of one or more individuals in the workplace, or a professional recruiter, understanding these styles of behavior must absolutely become one of your 'tools of the trade.' Just view this book as your primer (and then you can come to me to dive more into the details and the benefits of such analyses). It will help you hire right the first time, manage much more appropriately and help individuals within teams work more productively and get along much more easily.

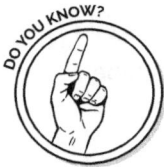

The 'I'—Do You Know Anyone Like This?

As I present the **I** style to you and describe the patterns of all strong **I** individuals in the next pages, do two things (just as you did when you read about the strong **D** patterns of behavior). First, see if you recognize yourself in any of the descriptions I give about the **I's** behavior style. Second, see if anyone you know (or know of, like a celebrity or any public figure) comes to mind as someone displaying these behaviors. Just like the 'ordinary' people we interact with every day, public personalities are an open book for us to read—so continue to watch for these patterns in all the people you interact with and observe.

Although the **I** style individual is very verbose and chatty, their listeners quickly notice a couple of things about their style. The first is that this individual excels at speaking in generalities. Why is that? The **I** style individual is very uncomfortable with details, hates research because it involves diving into the details, and when it comes to the facts, the **I** style person is very selective about which ones he latches onto.

Let's look at Lizbet, who is a very strong **I** style, at home.

Lizbet is happily married and the energetic, creative, chatty mother of two young children. Her household is happy, and the relationships she has with her extended family, and all her friends for that matter, are important to her. In fact, she gets along with all her family members quite harmoniously.

Now that both kids are in school, she has gone back to full-time work. Although she loves what she does and the company she does it for, she has a pinch of nostalgia for all the times she took her two young kids out to the park, played and rough-housed and had great fun together for hours at a time. It was the fun that she missed, truth be told. And although she's probably not conscious of it, being able to do what she wished with no eye on the clock suited her down to the ground. Now, in the evenings, she still makes sure to get some fun time in with her children and her husband. Luckily, her spouse has his eye on the clock and reins everyone in to get the kids in bed early enough so they get plenty of rest for school. Lizbet would probably be up with them at midnight if he didn't!

How can we most easily recognize an **I** style individual? That's a pretty easy—just look for someone with loud laughter, enthusiastically telling some sort of story or joke with fully animated body language and a big smile on his or her face! You have located a strong **I**! The strong **I** talks a lot, talks fast, moves fast in social situations (going from one to another without lingering). Not that the strong **I** behavior style is a braggart, but they do love to shine, be recognized before a group (watch for the group photos in which he has pride of place on his wall), and exert their influence. If you have spotted a people-pleasing extrovert, you have spotted a strong **I**.

Memory Jogging Words for the I—Is This You?

You can easily remember what describes a strong **I** individual's behaviors with some memory jogging descriptive words that begin with the letter **I**. Keep in mind that the strong **I** behaviors are much more multifaceted than just these words may indicate. But it is a good way to remember the primary indicators of the **I** individual. Remember that the **DISC** descriptive word for the **I** style is **influence**.

An **I** person is:

Interested, interesting *and* **influential** *(an* **influencer)**,
impetuous and impulsive, intuitive, illogical, involved,
interactive, inspirational, inductive, impressive/
impressionable, interrupters

Involved is a keyword for the **I**. **Interactive** is another key and you **I's** can mix and meet and start conversation even with strangers and be very comfortable.

Anytime people are getting together to do something, the **I** individual wants to be involved in the group. The **I** is willing to step up and generate enthusiasm and even entertain people as needed . . . as long as there is **interaction** and you let her be **involved**, she is happy to help and participate.

The **I** is not a planner, and will often just **interrupt** a conversation, or jump into a project or a task without thinking much about it beforehand, so we say they are **impetuous** and **impulsive**. Most strong **I's** are masters at verbal communication, and are naturally **inspirational** and **impressive**.

• •

QUICK QUIZ: Can you go back to the story about Lizbet, above, and underscore the descriptive words and phrases that tell us she is behaving from a purely I style?

• •

When it comes to making a quick analysis of the dominant behavior pattern of an individual, there are two quick ways to find out what his or her strongest behavior style might be.

Keep Up with the I

Your first clue that a person might be a strong I is about *speed*. The strong **I** person likes to keep moving at a fast pace. Everything about the **I** says 'speedy!' His mouth moves fast, too—all strong **I's** are very verbal. They speak quickly (and a lot) and seem to move like a whirlwind through their day. The **I** has a short attention span and thrives on a fast-paced existence which keeps him moving from one thing to another (and juggling lots of balls in the air) without diving too much into the details of anything.

Are I's Thing or People Oriented?

The second clue about this behavioral style is the strong *preference to be with and work with people* (not to mention having them as an audience, which the **I** craves). The friendly, strong **I** individual loves people! The **I** approaches most situations and interactions from a People Orientation. How can you tell if a person is strongly people-oriented? Easy! A strong **I** seeks out and is surrounded by people, and loves the interaction with them. The **I** simply likes everyone! The **I's** optimism and enthusiasm for life is contagious. Observe whether someone shares his enthusiasm and ideas with lots of people—that's an **I**. The **I** sees the best in all people and all situations. An **I** is the very illustration of a chatty 'networker,' loving to meet new people and pull them together. As such, the **I** is the life of the party and really enjoys participating in a group both at work and at home or in the community.

Watch how people interact in various circumstances with peers, children, elders, subordinates or the boss, and with strangers—if you observe any of the above people-oriented behaviors, you might just be watching an **I** in action!

Let's go back to Lizbet, and view this strong **I** style individual at work.

Since both her children are now in school, Lizbet has gone back to work. She understood and agreed with her boss when he defined her role and the results the company expected of her. Lizbet is a lead generator for her company, which means that she networks in person, makes live presentations before large groups, and generally discovers which of the people she speaks to are potential buyers for her company's products. She is consistently able to connect with her listeners and not only entertain and enthuse them, but get them so excited about the company's products that they are begging to buy. Her boss says that Lizbet is great at stirring up 'lust and desire' in individuals so that their only option is . . . to buy!

You Might Be an I If . . .

As I have noted, not all behaviors of this style are described by words beginning in the letter **I**—that would be far too easy and, really, one-dimensional. Let's layer this behavior style, but keep in mind that although I seem to present all of these characteristics and traits as belonging to a single individual, there is no 'all-**I**' or 'pure **I**' person out there! We are just collecting all the ingredients that *could* go into making a person a strong **I** style. Everyone has other styles to some degree, and the personal combination of traits we possess from each of them makes us not only multi-dimensional, but unique.

Let me show you the **I** style in the next few sections. Hold in mind that you—anyone—can possess just one of these behaviors, or many of them.

A Snapshot of the I Style

You **I**'s are the quintessential optimist. You are positive and optimistic, most always 'of good cheer.'

An **I** loves people—they are the quintessential people-person. An **I** appears to be in perpetual motion, always keeping up a fast pace from morning till night. This fast pace also applies to the **I**'s love of talking—they'll keep going and going!

An **I** is a happy, openly cheerful and friendly person. The **I** is a natural motivator, a generally charming, inspiring and enthusiastic individual. Inspirational **I** is an influencer, able to persuade people to embrace innovation or a need for change.

You're a social person—friendly and enthusiastic, even extroverted. You prefer a casual approach when dealing with people. You're great with people, are highly verbal and love interaction. You have a knack for producing a lively, creative atmosphere. The strong **I** can be quite a passionate, witty individual—and can whip up enthusiasm in others in no time at all!

A fast pace suits strong **I's** perfectly. You **I's** like lots of variety and opportunities to express creativity. You dislike rigid schedules and routine (perhaps because you cannot see them as offering opportunities for creativity). You dislike detail work and are quite willing to leave that to someone else—you are much more a big picture person!

Although you might not be interested in taking a leadership role (even though you most definitely can), you enjoy the approval of the spotlight. Being on the receiving end of high praise, recognition and positive feedback is what all **I's** love.

You are a verbal person—happy to talk with others—and there is no such thing as a short conversation with you.

The **I** style has terrific people skills and thrives in any job in which contacting people, networking and 'schmoozing' or 'working the room' is needed. The **I** keeps moving (and in this situation, that is the point), never stuck in a corner in one conversation! Business-oriented socializing is the **I's** cup of tea. You are good at drumming up enthusiasm and other people find you quite entertaining.

You **I's** are great talkers, but not very good listeners! You'd rather hear yourself speak.

The **I** individual loves meetings for several reasons! **I's** thrive in groups, love to have an audience, and love to be creative—which is possible in some meetings if they are about finding solutions, innovating or brainstorming. You **I's** will call meetings at the last minute because you believe this keeps people's reactions fresh or spontaneous. Meetings are an important tool for the **I** because you want to allow everyone to speak out, speak their mind, give their ideas. The **I** employee is the one person who thinks meetings and work are (or should be) fun! Thus, you like people who are open and friendly around you in the workplace, and this means you encourage people to chat, brainstorm, participate and work things out verbally.

The **I** person is really uncomfortable with repetitive tasks because it feels so slow and dull to them, but even more than that, **I's** are uncomfortable with details. The **I** worker is not the one to drill down into or focus on details, create detailed reports, or do detailed research. Expect the **I** employee to be a big picture person instead.

The **I** individual, at the start of any new project, wants to know who's involved and will ask to work with other people— remember you **I's** love people and enjoy group interactions. The **I** personally thrives on change (because it represents moving fast) and is your biggest advocate before those resisting the change. **I's** are your best choice to motivate and encourage everyone else to embrace the required change wholeheartedly!

I's stay away from conflict, from perceived unfriendly or reserved people, and all kinds of pessimism. Just as a strong **I**

person tends to avoid confronting anyone with any negative topic or feedback, **I's** also fear social rejection. You **I's** want all people to accept you (and why not, since you love all people yourself!), and you are very appreciative of public or social recognition.

If you are not an **I** yourself, but have assigned an **I** individual to launch any new project, you can rest assured that she will connect positively with all the players, draw them out and win them over with enthusiasm and get everyone fully involved. **I's** are the consummate networker—if you don't have the people you need, ask the **I** to round them up. If you need someone to contact total strangers for a purpose, the **I**-style person is who you must recruit for the job!

The predominantly **I** behavior style individual—in the workplace and in social situations alike—doesn't have a really good handle on the concept of 'time.' Like Lizbet, they have a hard time determining whether that social lunch, that business meeting or other event has gone on too long. They have a hard time getting hard-and-fast appointment times right, including just arriving on the right day and time, keeping to a strict one-hour appointment time frame (which the strong **I** needs to remember has only 60 minutes!). Likewise, the **I** project manager has a hard time estimating the length of time any task within the project (or the project itself) might take. It is never that the strong **I** disrespects other people's valuable time! It's just a hard concept to wrap his head around, primarily because the **I** gets lost in being busy, talking to folks and getting overly involved in his own storytelling, making sure he meets everyone that has attended the event . . . and having fun.

Key Spoken Words and Phrases of the I Style

Always asking about other people, with questions starting with "Who?" is typical of the strong **I**. They want to know—Who is involved? Who is in this with me? Who will be attending this meeting of ours? Who are you thinking of assigning to this team?

You can hear an **I** in his voice: An **I's** loud voice ranges from happy lilts to outright excited acceleration of speech to loud laughter. If it sounds like a motor is running—it is. And the **I's** talkative tendency may just be where the phrase 'motor-mouth' comes from!

The quintessential **I**-style person considers himself quite humorous, a great story or joke teller and a generally all-around great entertainer. They have a story for everything—and are determined to tell it! They are, as you can tell, comfortable yet casual speakers and can make a stranger feel like they've known each other for a long time.

Hearing "We need your help," and "I'd like your opinion on . . . " gets **I's** excited. An **I** might often be heard saying something like this:

- "Thanks for getting me involved."
- "I'd love to work with you on that project!"
- "Let's get everyone involved in this project (brainstorming; deciding)."
- "I have just the solution and we can put it in place by working together."

- "It is not what you know, it's who you know."
- "People are more important than things."
- "Let's party!"
- "Let's get everyone together!"
- "Didn't I do great?!"
- "Let's ask everyone what they think!"
- "Come on, kids—let's have some fun!"

Social acceptance and approval—as you see by the query "Didn't I do great?"—is very important to the **I's**, and clearly, their biggest fear is social rejection. The **I** believes, and may even say, "Everyone should like me. I'm a nice person."

Comments by others that would describe the strong **I** individual:

- "He's always up and energized."
- "She's so cheerful all the time."
- "He has the attention span of a gnat."
- "She's always so careful to get everyone involved."
- "He never seems to finish what he starts."
- "Ask her—she would love to get involved."
- "I can never seem to get a word in edge-wise with him."
- "He sure has a lot going on."

Key Body Language of the I Style

I individuals always have big smiles on their faces, their eyes are wide or winking with happiness and excitement, and they laugh easily (you'll notice many **I**'s laugh more at their own jokes and stories than their audience).

Individuals of this style accompany their loud voices with animated body language—often using their whole body to make a point to others, or just to express their enthusiasm and excitement. They take up lots of space with wide arm movement and liveliness with their whole body as they tell stories or take the floor as speakers to a group, or just get very enthusiastic about a product or service they are presenting to a prospective customer.

The **I**'s are not stiff or formal—and that is why you'll see them so animated of voice and body. They also want to make sure to chat with everyone present, and so seem to have 'the attention span of a gnat' as they flit (some would call them 'whirlwinds of motion') from person to person or group to group.

Now you are better equipped to detect a strong **I** person. You are beginning to realize that there are ways to motivate and support such a style, as well as ways for you (the non-**I**) to get along better with the **I**, or to manage and motivate one if you are their leader, boss, parent . . . or peer. Think about the **I**'s you have around you, the challenges the relationship with them may have posed, and we will continue by learning a bit more about what to do to improve all your interactions together.

Demotivating, Discouraging and Distressing the I

The strong I individual is gregarious and outgoing, is generally liked by everyone, and will probably be the friendliest person you ever meet. Nonetheless, as with the other three **DISC** styles, there are some environments or circumstances that can discourage, demotivate, confuse and even distress, the cheerful and optimistic I individual.

Demotivating or discouraging the strong I:

→ Jumping coldly right into business is not appealing to the I; he needs the chit-chat first.

→ Obliging this I employee or manager to work with or interact with unfriendly people, or shy and reserved people.

→ Requiring the I to do something all by himself without the input of any group—in other words, not benefiting from any interaction at all—is highly distressing to the strong I.

→ Dealing with pessimism or apathy in other individuals.

→ Needing to work out the details of any task or project on his own.

→ Making the I adhere to a rigid schedule or routine—or 'watch the clock.'

The I individual simply does not understand where unfriendly or quiet people are coming from, and it's disconcerting to the I to try and figure them out. Likewise, we have seen that the I thrives in gathering people around him, working in groups, and getting input from every individual in that group.

Recall how optimistic the strong I's outlook on life really is. Because of that natural rosy and upbeat outlook, pessimistic or apathetic individuals confuse the natural I—they can't figure out how to act, though their first reflex is to cheer them up.

The strong I individual, as we have seen, is not detail- or task-oriented—preferring to create a big picture vision and involve other people in any project. An I doesn't just *seem* to be avoiding details, facts or specifics—she is! Don't ask an I to do much planning, since planning involves details. Requiring a strong I do so is very demotivating, and he will be confused as to how to even go about it. The strong I's tendency is to disregard the clock; they hate time constraints and are not really good at time management.

What Motivates or Stimulates the I?

By now, you can probably name a couple of environments or circumstances that the strong I-style individual finds stimulating and pleasant! Let's look at what excites or motivates this style, so that we can provide more of it to them.

→ Events and surroundings in which the **I** can chat, socialize, network . . . and talk and talk.

→ Make it fast and fun! Telling the **I**, "Have some fun with it" or "It will be fun!" and "Just run with it" is just the ticket to motivating him.

→ Being involved with a group of people who are gregarious, optimistic and creative is his perfect group, because the **I** is group-oriented and social.

→ Being given opportunities to dialogue and interact with others is just what he loves.

→ Make sure you express positive kudos, present any award or congratulations enthusiastically and in a public or group setting.

→ The strong **I** individual speaks before he thinks, and is quite creative and innovative, so put that individual in circumstances where brainstorming, innovating or creating 'off the top of your head' is welcomed.

→ Give redirecting or positive verbal feedback to the **I** right away—but in private.

→ Let the **I** express feelings and spend time with others who need/want to as well, and give opportunities for the **I** to verbalize ideas and thoughts as they arise.

→ Recruit the **I** as your ally in presenting the need for change to the groups of people it affects.

Let's go back to Lizbet on the job.

Lizbet's boss is **DISC**-trained and fully understands what makes Lizbet 'tick' from her strong I perspective. He doesn't perceive 'positive' or 'negative,' but has learned when to let her 'do it her way' and when to give her structure and guidance. That's why he has assigned her a non-I-dominant assistant.

He knows Lizbet will have no consistent expertise with the details that the company nonetheless needs from and about these leads she has collected, but her assistant is aware that his job is to 'vacuum up' as many details and commitments from those prospective buyers as he can. He thus steps in to collect contact data from interested buyers, and to put the internal sales process in place for each of the leads Lizbet has created. Her boss has mapped this support out for her, and rationalized it as a way that Lizbet can do more of what she not only loves, but what she does best.

Lizbet loves this work, and feels that it is a good fit for her ability to communicate, to excite people for a certain purpose (to buy), and create bottom-line revenue success for her company. In his observations and in comparison to others who have done the job before her, the boss knows that Lizbet connects with 4 times more people than any non-I. Amazing what you can achieve with the right person in the right job!

The boss's approach with her has paid off big time: Since Lizbet has come back to work, and directly due to her work, the company has 250% more qualified leads for the sales and customer care people to convert to buyers—and she's done the job so well that 90% of those prospects do indeed buy from the company!

Talents and Careers of the I

When considering career paths for a strong I-style individual, remember that the **I** typically exhibits:

→ People orientation
→ Verbal/language mastery, with ability to excite, inspire and motivate others
→ Ability to get groups of people working together or enthused, fully involved and participating
→ Optimistic outlook and friendly good cheer
→ Big-picture visionary
→ Creative and innovative
→ Comfort in fast-paced environments
→ Multi-tasker

I-suitable jobs will offer:

→ Lots of interaction with the public
→ Opportunity to chat
→ Opportunity to choose one's own fast pace
→ Few structural or procedural constraints

Specific careers for the **I** style:

- → Performance arts—actor, TV or live show presenter (announcer), comedian, dancer/choreographer, musician (a rock star!)
- → Party or event planning
- → Master of Ceremonies, hostess/host or greeter
- → Tour guide
- → Athlete, stuntman
- → Marketing, advertising, public relations
- → Receptionist, cashier
- → Childcare worker, counselor, social worker
- → Journalist or interviewer
- → Public speaker
- → Teacher
- → Workshop facilitator
- → Direct business-to-business sales, or business-to-consumer selling such as in an open-air market
- → Sales agent (real estate, insurance—networking and/or presenting in person to prospects)
- → Property manager
- → Team facilitator/leader
- → Litigating attorney

Do's and Don'ts for I's

By looking at four patterns of behavior—the **D, I, S,** and **C**—you can see that people who are not your own dominant behavior style will act or react in ways that you don't expect. That is because of our very human tendency—which we are dropping, I hope, little by little, as we absorb these behavior styles and the patterns within them—to expect others to do things the way we would. They don't. It's a fact of life.

Knowing how others behave, what motivates them, what their strengths tend to be and so on, you are better able to gently adapt and modify your expectations and do some things (while avoiding doing others) that help you get along better.

As I have said in a number of different ways, the **I** loves people, likes to keep going at a fast pace, and is an excellent motivator of individuals and groups. But who motivates this motivator? That is what you need to learn to do if you have an **I** in the family or on your work team! Start with these clear-cut Do's and Don'ts with the **I**-style individuals you live and work with.

Do This

Provide plenty of opportunities to interact and talk with people. The **I** doesn't need to be the leader, but does require being in a group to thrive.

Give feedback or ask for improved or corrected work in

private—on a one-to-one basis—with all **I's.** They want to be liked by everyone, and getting their fingers slapped in front of others is a morale-killer for strong **I's.** They believe that people will like them less if they are shown up in this way.

Let the strong I-style people multi-task. They like to move from one thing to the next (and make sure other people are involved, too, as I said above!).

Ask the I to help when you need to make any change in your company or organization or in how any project goes. The **I** is the perfect persuader, and can best drum up buy-in and enthusiasm for the new direction you need everyone to take.

Don't Do This

Withhold public recognition. When announcing kudos and congratulations to the I-style person for a job well done or when granting any award, make sure lots of people are around (even informally) to hear about it.

Make the **I** work alone, because his productivity, effectiveness and general enthusiasm will disappear.

Require detailed planning or research to unearth details about any topic. The **I** is not exactly 'allergic' to details, but gets flustered and confused when faced with a need to produce any! The same goes for facts. Give detail work and fact-finding to someone else.

Ask for any sustained, focused efforts. The **I** is just not that person, as it requires them to slow down, and they don't care for that at all!

Ask an **I** to closely manage his time. When networking, public speaking, arriving for meetings—the **I** will need some discreet but firm assistance to start and stop on time, to arrive and leave on time.

Key Strengths of the I

The strong **I** individual gets along with everyone, is kind, cheerful and optimistic. Creating and maintaining high morale in groups, loosening tension or stress with a bit of humor or a story (told with energy and enthusiasm) makes **I**'s welcome on many teams dealing with heavy workloads or working short-handed or just stressed out for any reason. For this reason, although you the reader may not believe that the strong **I** has any desire to be a leader, the **I** can and indeed does take on leadership roles with great panache! They keep on motivating and bringing the team's enthusiasm back to the task at hand, which many times is all that a group of skilled people need.

I's can generally 'turn on a dime' when the need for change arises and are encouraging to others in such times. They can charm their way out of many a tight spot.

Ideas born of their natural creativity and innovation, along with enthusiastic energy, are the **I**'s 'claim to fame.' The **I** is great at getting projects started—they can drum up enthusiasm in teams or with stakeholders. **I**'s are great at brainstorming or developing new ideas—and getting groups to do the same. The **I** is a great and enthusiastic public speaker. They get along with most people and engage conversation very easily and comfortably, making total strangers feel like life-long friends in a few short minutes. This is great news for success for the **I** who has landed in the right career!

They are quick to calm down from any angry outburst, and quick to forgive-and-forget and to move back into their habitual happy outlook. They recognize feelings and emotions are part of human nature, and will give sympathetic support to someone in emotional doldrums.

A strong **I** will tend to have truly mastered social skills, and will lean heavily on them to accomplish his goals. Relationships are vitally important to strong **I's**, and they will do almost anything to make sure that happiness and harmony reign in all their relationships. Should disharmony or malcontent surge up, one of their fortunate social skills is to turn on a dime and to flip situations around with a quick repartee or smart explanation.

Weaknesses of the I Behavior Style

The strong **I** individual can be so enthusiastic that you will be seen as a showoff. The **I** tends to exaggerate for the sake of a good story. But when others perceive that you stretch the truth for the sake of a mere story, they may fear they cannot trust what you say in more serious circumstances, either.

The **I's** verbosity might be an irritant to quieter individuals. The **I** is a loud speaker who will interrupt others because (in others' opinion) he likes to hear himself talk—that is how he grabs attention, and the I indeed loves to be the center of attention. They are simply hard to shut up!

I's can be gossipy or prying and intrusive (often because it is hard to get a word in edgewise with them or to just walk away from them). The strong I's impulsiveness, combined with the tendency to talk, talk and talk some more can lead the I to saying things that are hurtful to others. To his credit, the I is quick to make amends. They are quick to anger, but likewise to their credit, it never lasts long.

Although they do everything they can on their side to avoid interpersonal conflicts, the I's have an unfortunate tendency to talk before they think and to generally be quite impulsive and spontaneous in word and deed—all of which might end up offending and hurting someone's feelings, disrupting a process that is underway, or taking undue risks.

Strong I individuals won't be good at following through on commitments or sticking to a strict timeline. They are not good at implementing new ideas from start to finish—it is the finishing up aspect that eludes them! The I does not excel at completing projects on a high note or on time . . . or at all. Their sense of time is all over the map. I's don't attend to detail work or planning, and thus won't think things through enough to prevent missed deadlines, negative consequences or undesired outcomes. They may use facts and data selectively to fit their own needs rather than the realities of the situation, going on intuition to make decisions instead.

As eternal optimists even in the real, harsh, data-driven world of work, strong I's may project overly rosy results for a project.

This is again due to a short attention span and a dislike of process and details. The **I** does not like rigid rules or to follow rigid procedures.

The **I,** naturally impulsive and curious, open to change and risk, can be unpredictable.

And if you as a strong **I** parent or workplace supervisor are facing a situation where discipline is called for, you are likely to be a softy about it! Your child will see it as a benefit, no doubt! Your spouse or the other siblings probably will not! The **I,** in other words, can be overly permissive—and of course as a manager or parent that can backfire more often than you would like! The **I** is 'a softy' because he wants everyone to continue to like him . . . not always the best motivation for not doing the right thing.

If you are the **I,** you must develop a stronger self-awareness of what others perceive as negative qualities in you. Knowledge of your behavior styles and self-observation helps you to counteract these perceived weaknesses, perhaps turning them upside down and making them benefits and strengths.

Your excessive enthusiasm, high-speed verbosity, lack of structure and short attention span may lead clients and coworkers, as well as members of your hierarchy, to believe that all those behaviors are a smokescreen for your lack of skills, talents and abilities! If you are this **I,** you would do well to keep their perceptions in mind, and to dial back these tendencies when you are persuading bosses, team leaders, clients and company executives that you indeed do have the knowledge, skills and abilities that you are presenting. "Think before I speak" and "Plan before I do" should be things you continuously repeat to yourself!

Are I's Extremes Good or Bad?

People who are the opposite styles of the predominantly **I** individual—and for all strong **I's**, that is the strong **C** behavior style (read about that in one of the next chapters)—will view the gregarious, chatty **I's** as annoying, loud, frivolous, too verbose or gossipy or just plain full of themselves (since the **I** hates to be interrupted, while joyously interrupting others)!

Because the **I** is loud and more or less always in motion and talking, non-**I** style individuals might feel . . . exhausted! This might cause people to flee the **I** and look for peace and quiet elsewhere. If your young child (or close co-worker) is such a strong **I**, then you probably know the feeling!

Opposites to the strong **I** will also be unhappy and worried about his or her lack of reliability or dependability (since they flit from one thing to another), their lack of discipline (since they have trouble with follow-through and completion of projects) and disorganization (due to the **I's** dislike for detail and structure).

Are these extremes? It is a personal judgement that you make based on the situation at hand!

I's Extremes

The strong **I** behavior style has some quite predictable and visible elements. We refrain from judging any of them as good or bad, positive or negative. These are simply the styles which are naturally preferred by individuals displaying a strong **I** style in the course of any normal day. No matter who we are, each of us ratchets up some of our normal behaviors in times of stress, an emergency situation, a crisis to be immediately managed, decisions to be immediately acted upon. The **I** is no exception whatsoever!

The talkative **I** can, for instance, be greatly entertaining and fun-loving. However, in times of great pressure the **I** might ratchet up his natural talkative nature and verbally attack others, aggressively interrupt others and appear pushy in order to fulfill some agenda. When things calm down again, so does the **I**, by sliding back into friendly, optimistic chattiness. See if you can identify which of the strong **I's** natural behavior styles are ratcheted up, as you read this short list of extreme behaviors:

→ Undisciplined
→ Late (time management issue)
→ Doesn't know when to go home
   (time management issue)
→ Sucker
→ Reckless risk-taker (detail and planning
   avoidance issue)
→ Boastful
→ Prying/Pushy

The I—Is This Someone You Interact with?

The **I**'s sometimes enthusiastically overpromise, and chances are that it was a case of 'speaking without thinking.' If you are this **I**'s boss, help the strong, overpromising **I** to dial back on promises made to prospects or customers (and even coworkers), by for instance requiring him to add two days to all proposed delivery dates. Or no longer offering discounts spontaneously to woo a prospect, but instead have the **I** surprise a client with one (that you have previously approved) on the final invoice. Come up with some approaches that work for both the company and your **I** employee. It will save embarrassment in the face of unhappy clients, the need to re-do work, and the frustration to the **I** of being called to task for mistakes.

Interacting Successfully with the I

According to what you now know about the **I**'s style, do you have a strong **I** style individual at your office or at home? If so, then you notice that they love to talk about anything and everything—as though their own voice is music to their ears. They tend to pull groups of people towards them as an audience. They are the loudest and most animated person in the room.

Instead of interrupting them (to participate in what will really go back to being a one-sided conversation), your best approach is simply to nod and listen to what they have to say.

At home and at work, you'll need some approaches to manage this strong **I**. Be aware of how to manage the **I** if you are discussing with her the pros and cons of some decision you need to make jointly or by consensus. You'll need to stop your strong **I**'s stream of consciousness briefly and frequently to get her back on track, discussing only the topic at hand. And then when the conversation is completed and you believe you have made some kind of joint decision, it is a good idea to clarify what was decided with your **I** person. Why do you need to do this? You remember that the strong **I** style individual is not much on details, and will flit easily from one topic to another, due to his shorter attention span. You'll need to make sure the **I** has captured the decision and any details that he needs. Also keep in mind that the **I** is more intuitive and spontaneous than fact- or research-oriented in much of his decision-making, so your brief and pointed interruptions will also be needed to keep the **I** in touch with reality!

To help the **I** arrive on time, have an assistant give her a call that "It's time to leave for that appointment now." Sometimes it helps to tell the **I** a tiny white lie: That the meeting is scheduled for 2:15 pm, when it really starts at 2:30. You might have hopes of getting your distracted **I** there on time!

If you are coaching, supervising or parenting a strong **I** individual, keep in mind how social they are and how badly they want group approval. This means that if you need to give negative feedback, to criticize or correct their actions or work in any way, you best do it in private. When you must call him or her to task, provide guidance, or firmly help the strong **I** to get organized—do it on a one to one basis only.

Some of the feedback you might need to give the strong **I** may concern following through on projects that began well, but are faltering. It may concern ineffective structuring or planning for a project or some kind of assignment or task. The **I** may see 'mapping out' or structuring a project as 'detail work' and avoid it for that reason—so make sure in the workplace that someone else is asked to do that (or sit and do it with the **I** yourself). Or it may simply be that the strong **I** individual is putting off getting started in the first place, flitting around instead from one other project to another. Remember that the **I** is not a natural follow-through worker, and not a great detail implementer.

Also remember that the **I**'s response to most projects or problems is "Let's ask everyone what they think!" or "Let's get everyone together on this!" If you really need the **I** to firmly decide all on his own rather than get a group consensus, tell him—and hold him to it. If you really need the strong **I** to break down her solution into action-steps (details, in other words), tell her—and hold her to it. Or better yet, sit with the **I** as he or she does it alone, and give encouraging support for progress!

To get along with **I**:

> → Smile at the **I** when she is talking to you. Eye
>   contact reassures the **I** that she is the center of
>   your attention, which the **I** craves.

→ In your parental, supervisory or peer roles, don't yell at or lecture the **I**—in the case of conflict, disagreements or poor performance, just openly talk through any problem you have with him, one on one, and keep it specific ("People are complaining" is too general; "Kendrick and I have noticed . . . on every Thursday . . . 10% . . . " is specific).

→ **I's** like to hear your stories and ideas, too. The **I** interprets your silence as 'you don't like her' . . . so interject questions and comments every so often, even if it seems forced to you. A great way to get along is (if you are personally shy or just not much of a talker) to ask the **I** some question to get her chatting, or to make a brief comment to the **I** every so often. The talkative **I** will quickly take over the conversation and you'll be off the hook!

→ The **I** learns best by doing the thing directly or by observing others do a thing. When bringing something new to the **I**, don't just sit him down with a manual. Give a demonstration!

→ Remember that the **I** loves sincere and enthusiastic praise and kudos, and an audience to hear you give it to him!

What If I Am Not All This One Style?

I can almost guarantee that you are not just this one **I** behavioral style, no matter how much you resonate with it! That remains true, even if the **I** style ends up defining your strongly dominant behavioral pattern.

Just as with each of the four behavior styles we are discussing, there is no individual who is only of the **I** style. I am laying it on thick for you, so to speak, so that you can discern the **I's** style with crystal-clear clarity. When you have read about all four styles, and perhaps identified yourself or others you know in each of these styles, go to the later chapter which shows you how each one combines with other styles to make each of us quite a unique individual.

Just for Fun

→ Favorite question: Who?

→ Favorite color: Red

→ Favorite animal or pet: A fluffy, rambunctious, playful puppy

→ Preferred car: Any convertible

→ Oft-repeated motto: "Lighten up!"

→ Distinctive song: "Celebration!"

→ Life philosophy: Let the good times roll!

→ Preferred magazine: People

→ Target: "Ready . . . Aim . . . Talk!"

→ Top two needs experienced by the strong **I**: recognition; interaction

In Summary

Of the four **DISC** styles, the **I** behaviors, motivators and strengths make them the most gregarious, talkative, friendly, inspirational and influential of all the styles. The **I** believes we can have fun both on the job and in our leisure time, and thinks the rest of us should 'lighten up and let go' more often!

I's are outgoing, social, energetic and talkative. Very talkative! It is how they connect with people, innovate and create. They like to be the center of attention in groups and, conversely, don't like to spend much time alone.

They don't need to be the leader, but will take the lead to gather a well-motivated group together to launch any program or venture you set forth. They are great at getting people together in view to launching projects and getting things started with great energy, but will not be the person crossing the finish line. You can count on their innovative creativity to bring a big-picture vision to the overall project and to be the consummate multi-tasker you need to move it forward.

I's prefer to move fast, and often 'intuitively' feel inspired to jump into a task without weighing the consequences or assessing risk. This said, in case of a failure, the **I** is adaptable and quick to change directions and try again . . . but will surely be just as (enthusiastically) disorganized and unstructured as the first time around!

I's <u>succeed</u> due to being positive, energetic, enthusiastic, and using their masterful social skills to generate discussion and ideas from people in groups. They are very good at generating a team's excitement to move toward a goal . . . together. They are not only networkers for their own sake, but enjoy connecting people to each other (their influential and inspiring side).

I's might <u>fail</u> due to carelessness (sometimes to the point of sloppiness), impulsiveness, a lack follow-up or completion. **I's** don't like details and don't care about collecting or correctly using supporting, factual information. They tend to base decisions on their intuition and emotion, and typically remain optimistic about the outcomes of those decisions . . . and this approach can lead to failures. They prefer to make the popular or favorable choice, rather than the hard or difficult one (which is fact- or data-driven).

I-style people are quite perceptive about other people's emotions, and when those feelings are negative, will often step in to give support or just listen for a moment. An **I** is great at restoring morale, good cheer and optimism! He is not, however, good at achieving any kind of lasting resolution to an issue. This said, once an **I** has helped calm people down and walked away, at least those people now have cooler heads to resolve things themselves!

In a strictly organized work environment, the strong **I's** might be perceived by their focused, efficient and hard-working coworkers as quite unproductive and unfocused, flitting here and there between tasks and finishing none.

Non-**I's** often admire this **I** style of individual for their unshakable optimism and outgoing behavior. Ideas and enthusiasm are the **I** trademark. As a people person, **I's** love chatting with folks, and see the best in all people and all situations. The **I** is a perfect networker, quite comfortable and happy to meet new people. **I's** love pulling people together, having people around.

In groups, you are the lively one. You love being the life of the party and the limelight, but don't need to hog it—you love to get others involved and participating, too.

Are you this **I**? Maybe a little bit. Maybe a lot! Maybe not at all. Read on to discover the remaining two dimensions—the '**S**' and '**C**'.

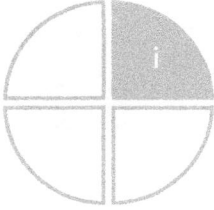

Chapter 6 bis

*Charting the I
Behavioral Style*

I's Top Observable Characteristics

1. Accepting
2. Active
3. Adaptable
4. Animated, spirited
5. Cheerful and optimistic
6. Demonstrative, excited
7. Dreamer and innovative visionary
8. Emotional
9. Energetic and enthusiastic
10. Fast-moving—a whirlwind of energy
11. Flexible
12. Generous and trusting
13. Impulsive, spontaneous
14. Independent
15. Influencing, persuasive
16. Interactive and sociable
17. Popular, extroverted
18. Risk-taker, adventurous
19. Self-promoting
20. Talkative

I's Typical Body and Verbal Language

Body

- Animated body—arms, hands, face
- Big smiles
- Energetic
- Occupying lots of space
- Whirlwind of motion

Voice

- Always asking, who?
- Cheerful
- Entertaining story-teller
- Laughter
- Loud and quick (speaking voice)
- Master of the spoken word

Basic Motivations

- Approval
- Freedom from time constraints
- Getting everyone together
- Popularity
- Public recognition

Environmental Needs

- Chance to verbalize ideas and show creativity
- Friendly relationships
- Opportunities to influence, enthuse and inspire
- Prestige

Best Leader the I Can Work for Is One Who

- Creates, or allows the eye to create, an atmosphere of excitement and enthusiasm
- Is democratic and friendly
- Offers group work or group interaction, inside and outside work
- Provides incentives for risk-taking
- Provides public-forum recognition of abilities and achievements

What the I Could Learn

- Accountability
- Active listening skills
- Awareness that enthusiasm and over-optimism can and must often be dialed back for success
- Time management skills

I's Top Motivators

1. Acceptance
2. Approval, popularity, being the center of attention
3. Conflict-free environment and relationships, numerous harmonious relationships
4. Constant change
5. Creativity—opportunities to express feelings and ideas
6. Fast-paced work, lively environment
7. Flattery
8. Flexibility
9. Freedom from controls and details, rules and regulations
10. Friendly environment and people
11. Granted authority
12. Group work and activities
13. New projects or assignments
14. Open-mindedness
15. Opportunity to help and/or motivate others
16. Practical procedures
17. Praise, public recognition
18. Short-term tasks or projects
19. Spontaneity
20. Varied activities

I's Top Demotivators

1. Accountability to rigid schedules and tight timelines
2. Being around pessimistic people
3. Being ignored
4. Being interrupted and pausing his speech
5. Boredom
6. Demand for perfectionism
7. Dislike or unfriendliness from his group
8. Diving into detail
9. Doing routine tasks
10. Formality
11. Long-term tasks or projects
12. Micro-management
13. Monotony
14. Receiving criticism in front of people
15. Rejection of his ideas
16. Structure
17. Unfriendly or highly formal environments
18. Working alone
19. Working with critical or unfriendly people
20. Working with slower-paced people

I's Top Strengths

1. Adaptability
2. Charisma, charm
3. Creativity and curiosity
4. Delight and enthusiasm
5. Demonstrative and expressive of body and word, spirited
6. Friendly
7. Generous
8. Good sense of humor
9. Influencer, communicator, good on stage, storyteller, talkative
10. Inspiring
11. Interaction
12. Lightheartedness
13. Lives in the present
14. Optimistic
15. Outgoing, warm, social
16. Persuasive
17. Promoter
18. Risk taker
19. Sincerity
20. Trusting

I's Top Weaknesses

1. Boredom
2. Controlled by environment
3. Changeable disposition
4. Disorganized
5. Dominates conversations
6. Egocentric, egotistical
7. Exaggerates
8. Get distracted easily
9. Gets angry easily
10. Goal setting
11. Impatience
12. Impulsive
13. Inattentive to details
14. Restless
15. Situational listener
16. Sloppy
17. Time management
18. Trust people indiscriminately
19. Undisciplined
20. Unproductive

I's Top Extremes

1. Answering for others, speaking without thinking
2. Careless, inaccurate, reckless
3. Day-dreamer
4. Defensive
5. Eccentric
6. Emotionally attack and decide
7. Fearful
8. Forgetful, relies on memory rather than a task list
9. Gabby, self-promoting
10. Insecure, in a frenzy
11. Irresponsible, overpromising, overly optimistic, makes excuses
12. Manipulative
13. Naïve, phony
14. Obnoxious (nasty)
15. Shallow, silly, superficial, dwells on trivia
16. Undependable, unpredictable, jumping from one task to another
17. Unfocused, flighty, enthusiasm fades fast
18. Unrealistic
19. Verbal attacker
20. Weak-willed

Top Things to Do for an I

1. Be positive and energetic, build a favorable, friendly environment

2. Create incentives for following through on tasks and for taking risks

3. Develop a participative relationship: allow more time than usual, with time for stories, let them set the pace of the conversation, make time for connecting and socializing, for sociable activities

4. Gently guide them back to the topic, keep the focus on their vision and goals, support their dreams and intentions

5. Give them recognition, kudos and credit in a public forum

6. Provide ideas for implementing action

7. Put details in writing, find other ways to help them transfer talk into action

8. Show how the solution enhances their image and/or saves them effort

9. Stay in regular contact with them and make it clear that your relationship is still strong

10. Take time to be stimulating, fun, fast-moving

Top Things Not to Do with an I

1. Allow him to overpromise when it may hurt the team effort
2. Be cautious for every little thing
3. Be curt, cold or tight-lipped
4. Be impersonal or task-oriented
5. Be unfriendly or negative or short of time
6. Cut the meeting short or be too businesslike
7. Do all the talking
8. Drive to facts, figures and alternatives
9. Eliminate social time
10. Engage in personal attacks
11. Establish more rules
12. Interrupt him during his storytelling or any presentation
13. Leave decisions up in the air—do pin him down
14. Let him slide on sloppiness or disorganization
15. Make him do anything alone
16. Overanalyze the subject at hand
17. Take too much time getting to action items
18. Talk down to them
19. Tell them what to do
20. Waste time in "dreaming"

I's Fears

- Being Ignored
- Loss of Influence
- Loss of Social Approval
- Rejection

Top Tips for an I's Growth

The **I** style can benefit enormously by writing out personal growth goals and setting a timeline for achievement. The **I** will need an accountability partner.

Be credible. Exercise control over your actions, words and emotions. You can 'assign' yourself each of these four approaches: 1) Be less impulsive—for a whole day; 2) be more organized and neat—at your office desk or in the kitchen (you decide); 3) Concentrate on the task at hand, on following through until it is complete—keep pulling yourself back to it when your mind or body wants to wander (it is, indeed about mind-over-matter); 4) be more results-oriented—and start with that new project you were just given.

Weigh the pros and cons before making a decision. This applies to your own decisions, but to how you hear and evaluate ideas of others. Consider and evaluate *in writing* (to help you focus) any ideas from other team members. This helps you also deal with things (writing that list of ideas) rather than with people only.

Talk less; listen more—for more influence. A way of doing this will also improve your empathic and active listening: slow down and hold yourself right there with the person as he presents his thoughts, instead of wandering off. This, again, is mind-over-matter and helps you remember to slow down your pace for other team members whose natural pace is slower than yours.

Develop punctuality—deliver your promises on time and respect others' time; likewise, develop realistic deadlines for tasks. Write it down. Have a buzzer go off to keep you on track or have an accountability partner question you about progress. With that partner, develop a systematic (written!) approach to focusing better on details and facts.

Take responsibility for the whole team or group's reputation, its results and its productivity overall—not just your popularity. Take a logical approach and seek facts and understand their importance for your team's work.

Phrases to Use That Encourage I's Energy with People

- "Who can we get together to work on this project?"
- "Who would you like to have on your team?"
- "We are looking for someone with energy and enthusiasm like you!"
- "How soon can you pull together a meeting with everyone?"
- "Can you help me with some ideas to get this started?"
- "I'm so excited that we get to work together!"
- "You add so much fun to everything!"
- "What would be a good way to reward ourselves when we reach our first goal?"
- "Thank you for your positive attitude and outlook!"

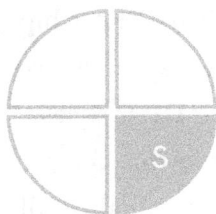

Chapter 7

Position Yourself in the Bigger Pattern: The 'S'

THE *S* in our study of behavior patterns set forth in **DISC** stands for *Steadiness*.

A Word of Caution

I would like to start here with a word about leadership and leadership styles as relates to the **DISC** patterns. As you read these pages, it may occur to you that one or another behavioral style is 'more suited' to leadership roles (and the related skills called decision-making and crisis management). That is not so. No dominant **DISC** style is a better leader than any other. Individuals who are dominant in any of these four styles might make a great leader. The question is only: What is that individual's leadership *style*? You will have seen clues to the answer in each chapter, but we will come back to this after I have presented all four **DISC** styles.

I must also remind you that I am describing in this chapter the nonexistent individual who has a **pure** (or as I will also call it, **strong**) **S** behavior pattern. This is simply for the purpose of helping you recognize all the ways an individual can display an **S** behavioral style.

Keep in mind that you and all individuals around you will possess one or more of the described **S** characteristics, behaviors, or motivations to a greater or lesser degree. A blend of all **DISC** patterns in each of us, which we combine according to our own unique recipe, is what distinguishes us from all other individuals. So now, let's see what the **S** style looks like in all its glory!

Where Are These S People?

The individuals displaying a strong **S** behavioral style make up 30-35% of the general population, and we need them for many, many reasons!

I will discuss it more in the next pages, but consider the economy of the society you live in. There is the public sector—the government and military. There are the agricultural, manufacturing or industrial sectors—that is where products of all kinds that we eat, buy and use are invented and made. Then there is the **service** sector, and that is where the **S's** are very likely to be found and to thrive. Because we all consume services, we need these **S** individuals in our workforce, active in our community projects, and able to render all kinds of services to us.

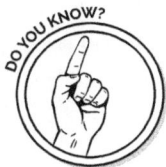

The 'S'—Do You Know Anyone Like This?

I invite you once again as you read the descriptions of a pure, strong (and totally non-existent) S individual, to think about people who are around you right now in your family, in your workplace, and who join you in all the activities you are involved in. Do you recognize any of these individuals' behaviors, tendencies or motivations as S? Which individuals around you seem to be more strongly S than any other behavior style?

Similarly, look at yourself as you read. Do you identify yourself in any of the provided S behaviors—in any of the natural or extreme reactions, strengths or weaknesses, motivators or demotivators, tendencies and preferences I describe? Keep in mind that each of us has a varying degree or 'amount' of this S style within us. Neither good nor bad, it is who we are today, and where we start when we have decided (as you see in the charts) to do some personal growth work on ourselves . . .

A strong S will have a tendency to be very helpful and get involved from the heart with people and projects that speak to his values. You might recognize the S's around you by their inability to say 'No!' when they are asked to help out in any way. You might also be looking at an S when you notice a calm and quiet, friendly person who seems to draw people to him like magnets.

Let's look at Eduardo.

Eduardo is a widower. His children are grown, with their own homes and lives. He still works in his chosen profession and is otherwise active, though he never seems to be in any kind of rush regardless of the number of things he is doing.

One of Eduardo's great joys is his activity as a volunteer in, today, three community organizations. His intention had been to lend a hand by working as a volunteer in a single organization. But he just doesn't know how to say 'No.' A friend got him involved in the second one, when Eduardo connected from the heart with its mission. It's the same with the third organization—he was approached to give specific kind of help that the organization urgently needed at the time, and, true to form whenever he is asked to help, he stepped in. He stepped in, but he also stayed, because he just thoroughly enjoys the people working there. He not only connected from the heart with the values, missions and programs of these organizations, he just loves that all the people involved give from the heart to make them successful.

His friends call his extensive volunteerism 'being roped in,' but Eduardo disagrees. If his wife were still alive, would he devote so much of his free time to this work? Probably! He just naturally connects with shared values, friendly people and the chance to serve with the skills he possesses—that's how he was when his wife was alive, too. He'd like to think that she knew him better than anyone and wouldn't have it any other way!

How do we go about recognizing a strong S-style individual? You look for a friendly, **service**-oriented individual, who is ready and willing to **support** you, your cause or organization, who is **sympathetic** to your needs.

Memory Jogging Words—Is This You?

The S in **DISC** stands for **Steadiness**. Another key to understanding the pure S is found in the word **Supportive**.

As with the other styles, it is easy to jog your memory with S words that describe the pure, strong S style. The **strong S** is not by any means *all* of these nor *only* these, but it will help you to situate people in this behavior pattern. These strong S behaviors will of course be much more multifaceted than any single word can possibly indicate.

Use this collection of S-word descriptions to begin to build a picture in your mind of the strong S behavior pattern.

Sideliner, self-protective, spectator, steadiness, supportive, stable/steady, sympathy, security, secretive, sweet, submissive/ sucker, shy, standards, status quo/sameness, sentimental, specialist, sharing, spectator, stingy, story-telling

The **servant/servile** memory jogger is about their tendency to feel or act on their excessive willingness to serve, help or please others . . . sometimes going over the top as they do so. The S has a hard time saying, "No, I won't help."

Specialist is important in the **S**'s career choices and skills development, and refers to 'technical' jobs as well. We'll have a look at the **S**'s best career or job choices later in the chapter.

Standards is meant in the sense of ethical values that the **S** holds dear. **Sharing** jogs your awareness of the **S** in the sense of sharing ethical values (like Edoardo's shared values with the community organizations he volunteers with), sharing skills, work or products or services they believe in, sharing of themselves through **stories** and memories and in numerous other ways we will look at.

Stingy may seem negative, but be aware of context before you judge! 'Stingy' for the **S** is meant in the sense that they like their own well-defined and familiar space, and the comfort of boundaries and possessions (including friends) that are familiar to them. They don't want to lose or give away (hence, 'stingy' or 'unwilling to give up') that comfortable feeling of **security**.

Smooth is another word that describes the **S**—they are typically very efficient with any familiar process or task; they are practical-minded and well-organized (if not always neat). These are people who **stay** within the lines, **stay** within a clearly-defined border and rarely go out of the boundaries in which they feel **secure**.

They don't want to hurt anyone's feelings, and this might put **S**'s in a bad position—when I say that the strong **S** could be a '**submissive sucker**,' that means they'll be led to doing something they don't really want to (submitting to it), just so that they don't hurt the other person's feelings. Someone might then say about the **S**, "What a sucker to fall for that." They feel it is more important to maintain the peace amongst people than to rock the boat.

The **S** likes to tell and hear stories, but unlike **I,** the **S** stays with close friends and family as their preferred audience.

Remember that not all strong **S** individuals display all <u>these</u> behaviors, but a good number of them will be evident . . . to the alert observer that you are becoming.

• •

QUICK QUIZ: Can you go back to the story about Edoardo, above and in the next pages, and underscore the descriptive words and phrases that tell us he is behaving from a purely **S** pattern?

• •

When it comes to making a quick analysis of the dominant behavior pattern of an individual, there are two quick clues telling you that his or her strongest behavior style might be the **S**.

Keep Up with the S

The first clue to determining behavioral style is through observation of a person's pace. The **strong S** will be moderately paced in all things. In this case, 'paced' might even mean 'measured'.

S's are easy-going and never makes waves in a group's way of doing things (as long as they understand what that is), due to **S's** preference for an even, steady pace and predictability in how tasks, activities and events unfold. In other words? If the individual you are observing is rushing around—you are not watching an **S**!

Are S's Thing or People Oriented?

The second clue to recognizing an **S?** Strong **S** individuals are people-oriented. In fact, I must more correctly say that they are *relationship-oriented*. For them, the phrase (turned upside down from its original form) 'It's not business, it's personal' might have been coined by the relationship-building **S**. They are the ones who get along with most everyone, but they will have a tendency to have very close relationships with only a select few.

They are sharing, caring and nurturing, open and empathic people. They are sensitive to feelings, whether their own or yours, and readily focus on other people's feelings, needs and desires.

They are verbal communicators, and deeply enjoy talking openly with others. They are happy to hear everyone's point of view and perspective. They like sharing stories about themselves, and want you to share your stories, too.

Now that you have a bit more insight into the strong **S** behaviors, you can continue your task of observing how people interact, work and get involved in the activities of life—and if you detect any of the above behaviors, you might rightly guess that you're watching an **S** in action.

You Might Be an S If . . .

Of course, not all behaviors of this S style can be described fully by words beginning in the letter S. That would be much too simplistic and one-dimensional—and as you are beginning to comprehend, no one is unidimensional!

So, let's begin now to create the layers that enrich this behavior style, while you remember that there is no all-S or pure S individual out there in spite of my presentation. These are just all the 'ingredients' available for the individualized, multi-layered 'recipe' that could become an S-style person.

A Snapshot of the S Style

The S is people-oriented—a relationship-builder—and likes to please others. This people-pleasing tendency can get them into trouble; the other three DISC behavior styles are there to push them around. When the S's feel that things have turned hostile or unfriendly, they might feel put upon by others and complain a bit . . . or even get angry. S's want to feel appreciated, after all!

You the S like the status quo. You like things to be orderly, organized and predictable, with clearly defined lines of authority and areas of responsibility.

S individuals are pleasant to be around because they give

the impression that they are able to see (and accept) things from everyone's particular point of view! And indeed, the **S** has the uncanny ability to do just that—even when all the opinions expressed are diametrically opposed. **S's** are the ones who will say to three people each presenting their divergent viewpoints, "You are right about that, Karolina, and so are you, Gustavo, and you are correct too, Mauricio." And they will mean it.

The strong **S** is there when you need him, listening, patient, understanding, accepting and loyal. If you have a friend like that, chances are he or she is a strong **S**!

They want to be needed by others, including their family. Although they'll wait on others, are great gift givers and are very nurturing, they like to feel that the effort is returned or at least appreciated in so many words. Remember to express gratitude and appreciation to that **S** in your family or on your work team.

The **S** is all about helping others, making things easier for them. If you have an **S** on your team, you probably won't need to ask—they're already identifying ways to be helpful for the project or the task at hand.

The strong **S** style individual may seem easy-going, but don't let that fool you about the **S's** strong values and standards. Ethical values are important to the strong **S** as a priority in their lives. Compassion? Justice? Ask the strong **S** what values they hold dear; they will definitely be able to tell you.

S individuals are dependable people who are comfortable inside a set routine or sets of rules, a defined space and a prescribed realm of action. They will do things in the standard tried-and-tested way when performing any task; they depend on sameness and shy away from change. They are not the ones who will be first to try something new.

The **S** may be a reserved and even shy individual, but do not underestimate them as excellent leaders! Although the pure **S** might be shy and prefer to stay on the sidelines or in the background or be the follower, the **S** can step up. Their style will be more of a coaching style, which for them means a 'democratic' style. They are willing to show others how or what to do rather than just tell them. If they are the top leader of an organization, it might well be a patriarchal type of organization, with the **S** leader taking care of his people and even helping them resolve their problems—kind of like a parent or patriarch might. They do have big hearts.

Bonding strongly but with only a few close friends is typical of the steady and fiercely loyal **S**.

The strong **S** individual can be overly modest, but they are naturally curious about people and have a dry sense of humor, saying funny things with a placid, calm expression.

The **S** behavior style, because of **S**'s love of security and stability and the 'known,' can become fearful and indecisive at times. They not only don't want to be wrong about anything (remember that they are people-pleasers), they see and accept as true so many sides to the issue that they cannot make quick decisions. So when you ask them a question? They might babble on with 2, 3 or more different answers—hoping to give you what they think you want to hear! They'll give all their thoughts on the matter to you . . . and leave you to make the decisions.

If a pure **S** should appear selfish or even stingy at any time, it is probably to preserve their own stability and sameness. As you watch the **S**, you might perceive that he is only protecting his own interests, and looking out for himself to the detriment of others or a group's plan. Remember that each strong **DISC** behavior style has its own way of responding when the individual feels he is losing control (or might do so) or is in any way thrown out of his comfort zone. The **S** is no different, and has self-protection mechanisms in place to retain or regain control and comfort.

Key Spoken Words and Phrases of the S Style

The **S**'s have friendly voices, rarely raised, even when they are angry. This can change when an **S** is feeling used or abused or pressured; then the **S**'s voice can be unpleasantly whiny.

Strong **S** individuals are great listeners, but are also talkative due to their love of sharing. The **S** likes to talk, and does so rather informally and comfortably. Does that sound like the makings of a great conversationalist? That nice person you had such a great conversation with at that recent event might be an **S**!

S's will be heard saying things such as:

- "How can I help you?"
- "What can I do to help?"
- "How are we doing this?"
- "How will we get it done?"

- "What do you (and you and you and you . . .) think about this?"
- "It doesn't matter to me."
- "Whatever you want to do is fine with me."
- "I'll be happy to go along with whatever you decide."
- "I can go along with that."
- "I have a place for everything, and everything is in its place."
- "Don't rock the boat."
- "I'll be there."
- "That reminds me of the time . . . " (The strong **S** shares. He has a large personal collection of favorite memories and stories, and is just waiting to tell you what they are!)
- "Let's be friendly and patient with each other."
- "Let's make things work through a team effort."
- "How can I best serve this company?" **

** This last comment is the 'secret sauce' for strong **S** people who are successful in any sales position! By asking _themselves_ this question even before asking their customer, they are very liable to win the sale. Why? The customer senses that the **S** salesperson has the customer's best interests at heart—and it is true!

Hearing "We need your help on this project, and here's your checklist of duties." gets you **S**'s enthused. You are likely to respond with something like, "I will help you in every way I can." The chatty **S** might just add something like, "But I think you should make these three decisions about the project first" or "But will I have enough time to think it through before I submit my work?"

An **S** will also start many comments with "This has made me feel . . . " and the **S** will go on to express the feelings that she has (be aware that the **S** may or may not be complaining or whining at this point!).

Comments Others Make about the S

Here are some things observers may say about a strong **S**, and although they sound both positive and negative, keep an open mind. Imagine the full context:

- "What a saint!"
- "I'll never understand why he lets his kids walk all over him. Doesn't he see how overly demanding they are?"
- "She's the best friend I have ever had."
- "She never has a mean word to say about anyone, and that makes me feel really guilty."
- "He's so insecure about his skills and competency in the workplace. He just doesn't know how to sell himself."
- "She is so whiny about her every ache and pain—I can't take it anymore."

Remember that whatever our **DISC** profile, all of us naturally expect others to behave like we do! Thus, the **S** who is so understanding, sympathetic, who seeks to help others and is such a great listener? He doesn't understand when others don't act like this towards him when he feels _he_ needs it, and he whines and complains.

Key Body Language of the S Style

No rushing around like a crazy person, and no large gestures for the **S**! Body language and speaking style both start from a reserved posture, and a moderate pace (although the **D** and **I** styles might say 'slowpoke!').

I am sure you have felt how some people radiate a certain kind of energy. An **S** projects an aura of calm, contentment and harmony.

Soft smiles, quiet laughter, a gentle touch with few gestures and deliberate movements define the **S**.

Demotivating, Discouraging and Distressing the S

The **S**, like anyone else, can be demotivated when in certain environments that run against the grain of their natural behaviors. They can be demotivated or discouraged in any of the following circumstances.

Change and all sorts of unpredictability unnerve the **S**. However, once the **S** understands that "The only thing that never changes is that there is change," he relaxes a bit. An **S** really needs someone else to clearly explain the reasons for the changes, the timeline for them (with, preferably, lots of time to prepare and adjust), and the processes that will be needed.

Aggressiveness amongst people the **S** is observing from the sidelines or against himself, will definitely disturb the **S,** whose natural response may include withdrawing from the situation entirely or stepping in to smooth things over. 'Aggression' includes competitiveness and confrontation in the **S's** mind. When pressured or pushed, the strong **S** may just respond by being angry or by feeling hurt.

Lack of support devastates the strong **S.** Working alone is like punishment for the **S.** Team and group work, done in harmony and with a shared understanding of the goals and processes—with everyone getting along—suits the **S** far better.

Naturally, the **S** will avoid uncertainty and disorder. If an **S** is on your team or in your family, and you know that a big change is on the horizon, help the **S** by providing lots of information about that change, why it's needed, how it will be beneficial to the group as a whole. Reassure the **S** that everything will return to a quiet predictable pace and order once the change is in place.

The **S** is demotivated, irritated or frustrated

> → When needing to work side-by-side with a fast-paced individual like their 'opposite,' the strong **D**
> → When they need to be assertive and take charge
> → When they are rushed and feel they have no time to review data, information or others' points of view—especially when it comes to decision-making
> → When **S's** do not understand *why* a change of any type is being pushed on them

→ When there are too many demands being expressed—they will just give up and give in, in order to get along

What Motivates or Stimulates the S?

Your biggest key in motivating the **S** is to remember how strongly they are relationship-oriented. Informality and friendliness are also keys. The strong **S** is content in harmonious groups or environments where others smile and are kind, not only to them, but to all others. They are at their best in calm and easy-going communication situations, and build rapport by showing interest in others—and by others doing the same with him.

In a work environment, your **S** staff are more comfortable with easy-to-follow, step-by-step instructions on what and how to do a thing (through a repetitive unchanging process), as well as being assigned to work in a collaborative group rather than all on their own. They love to hear, "We need you on this project," or "Can you help out here, please?" Give them the time and tools to perform good service. They are most at ease and productive when they have been assigned clearly defined responsibilities and tasks, and a clearly defined framework of authority or action. Allow for plenty of time—without rushing—for the **S** to do a task, complete a project or make a decision.

A desire for security, including job security (longevity in one position or organization) is a big reason that an **S** might have chosen your company or organization over another. Your business's consistent and predictable performance means a lot to them. They will do all they can to ensure your success, since their self-interest is involved!

Speaking of business, let's look now at some career choices that suit the **S.**

Edoardo started his schooling with becoming a physician in mind, but his love of animals led him to a very satisfying career as a veterinary doctor. He treats all non-farm animals. He owns but doesn't run his own clinic; he has hired a manager to do so. This allows him to focus on the pets and pet owners that come in for care. His business predictably keeps the same long hours each day; he believes that availability is a great service to his clientele. His fees are right in the middle of the spectrum in his region; he believes in giving value for money.

His great joy is 'interviewing' the pet and pretending to the owner that the pet has spoken to him about his ailments and recommended a treatment. That is how he connects to the owners in quite a delightful way, and he always encourages them to 'talk' to their pets. No pet ever snips or bites at him; he just has that calm, soothing way with them all. No matter how nervous or impatient the pet owners are, he is likewise soothing, and they leave a bit calmer than they came in. His thrust is always to improve things for other people, make it better, make it easier for them. People are comfortable confiding in 'Dr. Edoardo,' and even though pet owners can get a little crazy sometimes, they find that he is a good listener.

This career path has allowed Edoardo to earn a good living doing something he loves, and do it in a team. In addition to his very detail-oriented and efficient business manager, he always has two interns from the veterinary college nearby (his Alma Mater, to whom he is loyal and supports in this and other ways), and three vet technicians who serve both as receptionists and assistants in the consulting room as needed.

He loves serving people by caring for their pets. He knows how attached most people are to pets in the home (especially true of those who care for them medically as needed), and is happy to share his special skills and compassion with them.

Talents and Careers of the S

Every economy has a *"service sector."* This is where you'll find **S**'s, since **S** stands for ***Service*** for this behavior style! However, they are also great *technicians*. Indeed, if you think about it, much work that is called 'technical' or 'specialist' is actually a service job.

A pure or strong **S** is not excluded from the high ranks of company management, but the company will very likely be in the service sector in some way, as may be the **S** manager's role within it. As I said, the pure **S** will look for longevity, so will not be likely to take a position in a startup company, with little to no history to measure against. This said, strong **S**'s can be entrepreneurs at the head of their own company, and it will be a service-related or service-providing business 9 times out of 10.

Remember the strong S style's ability to see things from everyone's perspective, to create a harmonious atmosphere, and (as a people-oriented person) enhance and preserve relationships. The S has the qualities of soother, service-orientation, empathy and people-pleaser. If how I have just described the pure S sounds not only like a great fit for a service job, it also might sound just like a career diplomat! Indeed, work in diplomacy is tailor-made for the strong S.

Any 'job' where the S can stay for an entire career or at least for quite long periods of employment (the steadiness aspect of this style) is attractive to the S. S-style individuals are likewise great in any career in which you need a 'finisher.'

Look at the following examples of great career choices for the strong S, and you notice that they are specialists or technicians, typically operate or work in groups, and present a need to finish the task once begun.

- → Schoolteacher
- → Medical doctor, doctor of veterinary medicine
- → Medical technician, registered nurse, nutritionist, radiation therapist, nursing aide, therapist, dietitian
- → Front-line service people such as face or phone customer service representative, receptionist, bank or hotel clerk, child care worker, counselor, photographer, cosmetologist or esthetician, cashier, phone dispatcher, flight attendant or airport personnel
- → Retail sales clerk, other sales positions

→ Accountant

→ Intermediary or mediator

→ Bartender

→ Spiritual minister, teacher or missionary

Do's and Don'ts for S's

Each behavior style initially comes from a place of expecting others to 'be like me,' and as you are surely coming to understand—that is just not so!

Thus, if you have interactions with strong **S's** at all, you will benefit (as will they) from knowing how to gently adapt your natural behaviors and take into account the following Do's and Don'ts. Those **S's** all around you will thank you!

Notice how many of these approaches are great for work as well as family scenarios.

Do This

The basic <u>need</u> of the **S** type of personality is *appreciation*—and you will see many versions of this in this section! If you tell **S's** that you appreciate them, they quietly respond with a smile and a thank you. They feel good about you and themselves and will perform better on the job and generally feel not only valued but energized.

Be aware and attentive to their feelings. Like us all, the **S** can get grumpy or angry so just help them return to their natural sunny disposition by letting them know you understand.

Recognize the **S's** need to be helpful and join in. Do your best to provide those types of opportunities. The **S** particularly enjoys action in groups or work teams, but if you ask them to help one other individual, they are also glad to step in.

Help the **S** feel valued and valuable. Asking them to participate or help is a good way to achieve this. Thanking them for participation or a job well done makes them feel valued.

Heap appreciation on them for their great attitude, work or service, ideas and contributions. A simple 'Thanks!' goes a long way to help the **S** feel valued.

Realize that the **S** needs environments that are peaceful and interaction with groups which are harmonious, just as much as they crave approval and appreciation.

Understand that the **S** are determined to finish what they begin—they are finishers. Thus, for the best outcomes, give them plenty of time and resources to complete tasks and projects they have been assigned.

Provide workplace performance reviews, discuss complaints or criticisms that you may have of the **S** or his behaviors or his productivity, and prepare the **S** for change. BUT, do these things gently, calmly and quietly . . . and in private, as much as possible. A good approach with this feelings-sensitive style is the 'sandwich' approach: Tell them a good thing they have achieved and praise it; tell them something that needs improvement and state why it was not up to standards (**S's** get standards!) and suggest some specific ways the **S** can make those improvements; then close the 'sandwich' with another good thing you have to say and express appreciation for all the good work and all their willingness to improve.

Don't Do This

Don't let the **S** get too clingy, insecure, anxious or dependent. The **S** has a hard time being or working alone, or believing in his value—this is true. Instead, help them be more assertive, perhaps by reminding the **S** how smart, talented and strong they are in their own right.

If you can help it, don't abruptly ask the **S** to speed up, hurry or move faster (and you might do this because you are impatient with their moderate pace). Instead, make sure **S**'s know the deadline and why it has been set for that date or time, and how many people depend on the **S** doing his share of the project on time for best results. Ensure that they know the processes and procedures to follow, and start out well-organized to meet that deadline.

Don't suddenly change a method, process or deadline (especially to an earlier due date) without advance notice or warning. Instead, give plenty of lead time and explanations beforehand and make sure the changes are well understood.

Avoid publicly criticizing, yelling or shouting at the **S**. Conversely, don't gossip about or criticize others in front of the **S**. Instead, pull the **S** aside and make your point in private, with a calm voice and plenty of clear reasoning.

Do not ignore, mock or disparage feelings—not the S's, and not other people's. Instead, respect that relationship-focused S's see feelings and the expression of them as part and parcel of all interactions.

Don't feel too embarrassed by the S's repeated offers to provide help, by their gift-giving and other expressions of feelings like gratitude. Don't protest them, either! Offered by the S (as long as they are not overdoing it obsequiously), this is just how they fit in, build rapport, communicate and express themselves.

Don't take them for granted. An S is naturally generous with time, energy, conversation and small gifts, but likes to be thanked in return.

Key Strengths of the S

The strong S's greatest strength is helping—collaboration and cooperation in all contexts.

They are great at team building in a workplace context. Unselfishly providing service and helping are typical S contributions.

Faced with disagreements or disputes, the S's bring in their basic tact and diplomacy, their aptitude for fairness and hearing all points of view, their peacemaking abilities.

The S's are patient, collaborative, cooperative and helpful (making ready volunteers).

They are loyal to friends and all those they work with (as well as to the employer and the company's best interests).

More Strengths

- Accepting
- Calm
- Conservative
- Consistent
- Contented
- Good listener
- People-pleasing
- Reliable, dependable
- Respectful
- Tolerant
- Trusting

Weaknesses of the S Behavior Style

Like all four behavioral styles, S-style individuals' needs and tendencies can turn into weaknesses, and even represent dangers for the S-style individual.

Interestingly, given their aptitude for diplomacy, one of their biggest pet vexations is conflict and confrontation, which they avoid as much as they can. Why a weakness? Life is full of controversy and disagreements, and hiding your head in the sand doesn't change this! Better to take some control and act.

Perhaps due to their conflict-avoidance, the S style's greatest or basic weakness is lack of assertiveness. The strong S is someone who can be taken advantage of fairly easily, since he'll do something for you in order not to hurt your feelings (as he perceives them). Don't let a strong **S** that you know and love be abused or misused in any meaning of the terms! If your strong **S** friend is in an abusive relationship—personal or professional—make sure they get out of it, and get professional assistance to stay out of it. If they are being taken advantage of—financially, energetically, or in any other way—point it out to them, and make sure they get some help to turn things around.

This next weakness may seem to be the other side of that coin—they are used and abused on the one hand, yet on the other hand, they allow someone else to use or abuse themselves. I would call this weakness 'enabling,' where enabling is undesirable (for example by letting an ill individual perpetuate the illness). Again, if one of your loved ones is this strong **S** enabler, keep in mind that this **S** may need professional counseling to even perceive that he is negatively enabling another person.

On a less dramatic note, **S**'s are so sweet, and so happy when others are happy, that they might unwittingly set themselves up to get the short end of the stick. It can be as easy as, "Oh, let's have Edoardo do it," because you have been so selfless and generous before. An **S** will be taken for granted and others will expect those nice little gifts or the strong **S** jumping in to help to continue, without expressing any gratitude at all. This lack of appreciation cuts the **S** to the quick—they'll say they don't mind, but if this **S** is your friend, say or do something about this.

Are S's Extremes Good or Bad?

Any behavior style's strengths can pivot and become weaknesses when pushed outside your comfort zone or when you feel you might be losing control. The **S's** are no different.

The strong **D** behavioral style is the strong **S's** 'opposite' style. Thus, a strong or pure **S** individual might find that a strong **D's** behaviors and methods are over the top—rude or crude, blunt and uncaring—especially concerning the treatment of people. The **S** is shocked that a **D** would provoke or bring about confrontation, disagreements or deliberately (so it seems to the **S**) disrespect people's feelings and opinions.

The other styles' fast pace will exhaust the strong **S**, who prefers things at a more predictably moderate or even slow pace. A **D's** blunt speech and unilateral decision-making leaves the **S** with his mouth hanging open. Why? **S's** are people-pleasers and the **S's** style will naturally be to ask everyone's viewpoint and come to a collaborative, democratic decision. Conversely, the fast-paced styles become impatient and snappish with the slower-paced **S**.

S's Extremes

Extremes happen to us all when under stress or when we feel control slipping out of our hands.

As you've seen by now, the strong **S** behavior style has some visible elements revealing his **S** qualities to us, and some

predictable patterns of behavior. Good or bad, positive or negative? That is not what is important, since behavioral patterns
are context-driven for us all. What might seem to be negative
and counter-productive in one context is quite an assertive, re-
sults-producing action in another.

Like the rest of us, the strong **S** will ratchet up normal responses, behaviors and reactions in times of stress or pressure,
in an emergency situation concerning loved ones or people the **S**
feels a connection with. The **S** will also ratchet up usual behaviors
in order to manage some crisis.

The **S**'s easy-going, people-pleasing nature might lead them
to be nonassertive when they in fact should stand their ground or
speak out. They can be easily manipulated (even abused) instead
of respected, simply because they don't want to hurt anyone's
feelings or because they are so naively ready to help. The **S** steps
onto the sidelines from excessive shyness. What are you noticing
here? When the **S**'s have identified abuse, when they're feeling dis-
respected, when there is strong or heated disagreement amongst
those around them—our **S**'s react with an extreme version of their
usual behaviors.

The friendly and kind, sympathetic and sweet **S**'s might ratchet
up their natural behaviors when they become aware that they
have been taken advantage of, and express strong anger or visible
disappointment (sometimes with tears or other great emotion).
When the great listener who is the **S** has a problem himself and
needs someone to confide in, yet sees that no one is ready or
willing to listen to him, he may turn into a whiny complainer.

The natural strong **S** style will be a ready helper when you need a shoulder to cry on or a willing ear to hear you out. However, that can turn into an **S** who is dependent and clingy and possessive when the **S's** own needs are unmet.

The **S's** natural conservatism can easily turn into an outright rebellion against change or innovations. Self-preservation leads them to do things such as withhold necessary information or data, or stop working entirely. Or they might dig in to their positions (where they feel safer, and where they know the boundaries) and block progress or any change that makes them feel that their status quo is threatened.

S's will over-personalize professional relationships, and it can happen in several ways. They will get involved in others' feelings and try to soothe. They get into personal conversations about the others' families and often family matters, pets, hobbies, and so on. Such extremes can lead to chatting instead of working or becoming dependent and clingy of these people.

Now test how well you understand the S style's extremes. See if you can identify which of the strong **S's** natural behavior styles are ratcheted up to the following extreme behaviors:

→ Angry
→ Clingy
→ Complainer—whiner—martyr
→ Insecure
→ Intimidated or pushed into a state of fear
→ Nonassertive
→ Shy
→ Teary-eyed disappointment

The S—Is This Someone You Interact with?

When you understand where the **S** is coming from, what motivates or demotivates them, what their natural and extreme actions and reactions tend to be, you can adjust your own behavior style to help them feel at ease.

Here is one example:

If you have a strong **S** in the family or on your working team, watch out for indecision and insecurity. Instead of letting the **S** slip into dithering or clingy dependency on someone else's decision, talk them through all sides of the issue. You know they are good at seeing all sides, and that is why they cannot commit to one point of view! Ask, "Since you have great relationships with all the people involved, what is the one solution you just know they could all get behind?"

Help your **S** release his lack of assertiveness and decisiveness. It will keep him vacillating about making any decision. The **S**'s concern is that any decision be beneficial to everyone—a near impossibility, and why the **S** has such a hard time decision-making on his own.

Show the S that decision-making isn't life or death! Show him ways (when the time comes) to change his mind and take another direction. The S won't be as afraid to make decisions—or to jump into a change of viewpoint—when he realizes that 'being wrong' happens to everyone . . . and when he admits that 'you just can't please all the people all the time,' as hard as the S tries to do so!

Interacting Successfully with the S

Given what you know now about the S's style, think about that strong S individual you may have working with/for you or living with you. In both environments, as a work leader or a parent (or, let's face it—the spouse of a strong S), you will need some specific approaches to manage your interactions together.

Back to Edoardo, when his wife was alive and they were raising their children:

Edoardo's wife was the children's disciplinarian, and Edoardo was the kids' playmate. To get their father to do what they wanted, the children quickly understood (as children will!) that they only needed to tell their father, "Mom said it was okay to __, so come on!" Since Edoardo wasn't a fast decision-maker, his wife and his kids just took over that role. His spouse made sure she decided a healthy menu of meals; Edoardo was a pushover when the children wanted candy before dinner and he was fine with whatever his wife put on the table ("Isn't she a wonderfully creative cook?" he'd say). His wife kept track of the household repair list and maintenance schedule for the car, and made sure her husband just knew when he should put extra cash in the household allowance to pay the repair people she hired. Edoardo was happy to have a house full of his children's friends. It was his wife who sent everyone home with homework supervised and completed, and a big healthy snack to reward them for the job well done. He was more concerned about, "How do you kids like school? Do you have lots of friends? What's your teacher like?" than about their grades.

Did they try to reverse roles at first, with Edoardo as disciplinarian and tough role model for the kids? Yes. Frankly, it was a disaster fraught with great stress for both spouses! They came to the conclusion (really voiced by his wife, as you might guess) that honoring their natural behavioral tendencies was a more comfortable (and honest) way to manage things, and carried on quite happily after that decision.

I will grant you that, in many cultures, it is traditional that the father's word is law for the family, so to speak. The patriarch simply has the last word. The man of the house sets the tone and makes the rules. Well, we need to do a reality check on that tradition, don't we, and you have seen why! Given what we now know about three of the four behavioral styles, harmony may come from a different division of roles. When the man of the house is a strong **S** (and with 30-35% of all people being strong **S** types, and half of them probably male, that makes for a large number of male **S** family leaders), that does not mean he is not a good head of household! It simply means that inside the family, things get organized somewhat differently than might be traditionally expected (or accepted). It is neither good nor bad. It's just . . . different! And isn't that what makes life so interesting?

By now you understand this about the strong **S**: **S**'s thrive on being surrounded by people who need them, whom they can help to resolve conflicts or problems, especially when they are appreciated for doing so. Volunteering their services, skills, and building relationships comes very naturally, so when an **S** joins your team, make sure to assign them to a group right away. Communicating to the **S** that he is now a member of a 'special' organization makes him feel even more valued. Feeling appreciated is definitely high on the **S**'s list. Receiving appreciation from others, whatever its form—a simple thank-you for their work or helpfulness or insights, a handmade gift, token gifts like candy, an invitation—is not lost on the true **S**. Conversely, pleasing others—but also making others look good, by giving credit and kudos to those who deserve it—is just as important to the **S**.

Inside and outside the family unit, the **S** feels valued when invited to participate in democratic ("Let's find out everyone's viewpoint before deciding") processes. Imposing your point of view unilaterally may work, but only *after* you have asked for the **S**'s opinion . . . or *opinions*. Show the **S** that he is being heard and taken seriously, even when someone else's solution is chosen.

Another way to help the **S** feel at ease is to listen to him with empathy, understanding and patience. This is particularly important when **S's** feel they are in crisis in any way.

In groups or teams, **S's** are clearly an asset. They'll help you build team cohesiveness and motivate, help and coach their team to working together toward the goal. All strong **S's** value relationships, and will raise loyalty levels on the team as well as team cooperation and team spirit. They are great at working collaboratively with others, and like to feel that the team or group is unified in its approach and its goals.

In your interactions with the **S,** your grasp of his weak points will allow you to make small adjustments so that things go more smoothly. The strong **S** gets emotional under stress or pressure—for instance, getting stressful news—but will typically try to hide those feelings and the stress behind a smile. Our friends the **S's** tend to be oversensitive. They might take the blame for something not really their fault, or wallow in self-pity when it is not called for. **S's** who are overwhelmed might make excuses or complain, even whining their discontent. In any of these instances, invite the **S** to talk about it for a few minutes by saying something like, "I can tell you are a bit overwhelmed now," and let him know you are there for him; that is quite soothing to the ruffled **S.** Just make sure to not let the **S** wallow in those feelings for too long!

Lastly, remember that the **S's** are moderately-paced individuals, not whirlwinds. They just don't know how to hurry, move fast or rush! If you can accommodate that style, do so. You'll both get along much more happily. Just make sure that the **S** understands that mutually agreed tasks and deadlines are intended to be met.

Help the **S** get organized or write a step-by-step instructional process if needed.

What If I Am Not All This One Style?

While I can guarantee you that you will encounter many 'strong' **S's**, you need to remember that no individual you meet will be a pure **S** and only that. Even if the **S** style is the one dominant style for an individual, his behaviors will also include some of the other three patterns.

This is good! Life would be far too boring if people's behavioral styles fell into four boxes, and four only.

After describing to you the last of the four patterns—the **C**—I will show you how you can begin to discover the ways that these patterns combine with each other to enrich us as individuals . . . and to complicate our interactions with each other! Don't worry. It will be fun. And speaking of fun . . .

Just for Fun

→ Favorite question: How?

→ Preferred color: Blue

→ Most loved animal: Cat . . . teddy bear!

→ All-time favorite vehicles: Van, station wagon, SUV

→ Oft-repeated motto: "All for one and one for all!"

→ Songs that bring tears to your eyes: You Needed Me, Precious Memories, Will the Circle Be Unbroken

→ Life philosophy: "We can do it by working together!"

→ Preferred magazine: Us, Parents Magazine, Readers Digest

→ Target: "Ready ... Ready ... Ready ... "

→ Top 3 needs: security; appreciation; service

In Summary

Of the four **DISC** styles, the **S** behaviors, motivators, strengths, characteristics and qualities make them the sweetest, most helpful and supportive, most service-oriented, sympathetic individuals of all the styles.

Some visual signs that you are in the home or office of a strong **S** style person include a display of family pictures and memorabilia, bowls or trays of snack foods set out for anyone who is tempted, a general sense of informal comfort in the furnishings or layout of the space.

S's are gregarious, friendly and likable. They truly love people and are the best relationship-builders we have. They are great team players, and are the ones to call on to build harmonious teams focused on a shared goal. They are understanding, caring and always ready with a helping hand.

If they seem a bit slow and laid-back, they are not ill and they are not lazy—that's their natural pace and style. **S's** are not formal in speech or interactions. This style is informal, easy-going, humble—sometimes to the point of being too modest. The strong S style individuals are largely content with life in general.

S's are comforting, not confronting. Avoiding conflict is their motivation; appearing passive is the result, oftentimes. Though S's will often withdraw to the sidelines when conflict arises, they are nonetheless the perfect intermediary to diplomatically get everyone talking to each other again. The S enjoys helping others, comforting them—sometimes to the point of being an enabler.

As I stated in the early part of this chapter, any **DISC** style individual can take on a leadership role with success—and so can the strong S. In a leadership role, the strong S individual will be more of a coach or a democratic, collaborative leader sharing authority and allowing group decision-making. The S leaders encourage open communication, and will always be a listener who is open to all perspectives.

Choose an S for your leader when you have mature individuals or teams who need someone to listen to all perspectives, or when such experienced individuals or teams need to collaboratively make their own decisions about what to do and how. That others can make their own decisions under the guidance of the S is ideal, since S's typically have trouble coming to a quick and definitive decision on their own—they are far too open to all viewpoints to choose just one! They are cautious with unknown circumstances and not big risk-takers. The S values people and inspires their trust. They are not confrontational but know how to avert conflict.

In the workplace, S's are all about performing consistently and predictably, as much for themselves as for a boss, their own team or the company's best interests (not to mention its customers). They are good at creating a stable, happy workplace since that is their preferred environment.

S's discomfort with conflict sometimes prevents them from being honest and sharing their real thoughts, their real opinions and ideas. In such cases, people tend to take advantage of them and when that happens the S might need an ally to urge him how to rise up into his assertiveness and defend his own self-interest.

Because the S stands for steadiness and security, the strong S dislikes sudden change or innovations to a routine that rock their boat—this will be true both at home and at work. The change may be a new method or process to adopt, personal plans that change at the last minute, a sudden unemployment—any type of change can put a strong S into a tailspin. To alleviate the stress of a foreseeable change, notify the S's in advance and help them understand and accept it.

Non-S's often admire this style for their bright and positive outlook and belief in the best in people. They want to help others. All you have to do is ask.

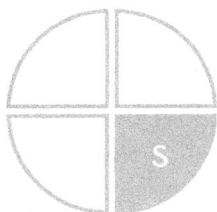

Chapter 7 bis

Charting the S Behavioral Style

S's Top Observable Characteristics

1. Agreeable
2. Calm, contented, patient
3. Conservative
4. Consistent, stable, status quo-focused, steady
5. Cooperative
6. Deliberate, reflective, systematic
7. Friendly, kind, soft-hearted
8. Great listener, soft-spoken
9. Loyal and reliable
10. Obedient
11. Possessive
12. Practical, realistic
13. Relaxed
14. Resistant to change
15. Security-oriented
16. Sensitive
17. Supportive, empathetic, understanding
18. Tactful
19. Team player
20. Unassertive and passive

S's Typical Body and Verbal Language

- A reserved posture
- A gentle touch with few gestures
- A moderate pace in all movements
- Deliberate movements
- Soft smiles
- Quiet, friendly speaking voice
- Informal speaking style
- Quiet laughter
- A whiny voice when ruffled

S's Top Motivators

1. Assistance in decision-making and clear direction/instruction
2. Being heard
3. Decisions based on causes and consequences
4. Established work pattern
5. Few arguments
6. Few conflicts
7. Finishing what is started
8. Friendly people
9. Help and assist others, team environment
10. Identification with a group
11. No sudden changes, given time to adjust in the case of change
12. Practicality of procedures and systems
13. Predictability
14. Private feedback, especially when negative
15. Recognition for loyalty and dependability
16. Stability, safety, sense of long-term security

17. Showed patience for their mistakes
18. Slow pace
19. Specialization
20. Tasks that can be completed one at a time

S's Top Demotivators

1. Argumentative people
2. Being in chaotic situations
3. Being in the spotlight
4. Changing the status quo
5. Cold, unfriendly environments
6. Competitive, aggressive environments
7. Conflict
8. Dealing with loud people, shouting or yelling
9. Impatient people
10. Insensitivity
11. Isolation
12. Lack of teamwork
13. New and heavy responsibilities
14. Precarious environments
15. Pressure
16. Requirement of a fast pace
17. Requirement of making quick decisions
18. Requirement to work alone
19. Suddenly changing direction
20. Work overload

S's Top Strengths

1. Ability to work in high detail work
2. Competent
3. Conservative
4. Cooperation
5. Dependable
6. Diplomatic
7. Enjoys routine
8. Finisher, completes tasks
9. Good listener
10. Helpful and supportive
11. Likable, friendly, kind, pleasant
12. Patient, easygoing, relaxed demeanor
13. Peaceful, peace-maker
14. Practical
15. Prepared, organized
16. Quiet, but witty
17. Reconciled to life
18. Steady, reliable, efficient
19. Sympathetic
20. Well balanced

S's Top Weaknesses

1. Averse to innovation
2. Avoidance of confrontation and conflict
3. Can't say no
4. Clingy and dependent
5. Easily manipulated
6. Easily taken advantage of
7. Enabler
8. Highly emotional
9. Indecisive
10. Insecure
11. Little assertiveness
12. Needy of support and a group all the time
13. Overpersonalize professional relationships
14. Possessive
15. Resistant to change
16. Selfish
17. Too involved in other people's feelings and stories
18. Whiny complainer
19. Withdraws due to shyness
20. Withdraws when hurt

S's Top Extremes

1. Clingy, dependent
2. Easily intimidated
3. Fearful of strangers
4. Feelings easily hurt
5. Indecisive
6. Insecure
7. Lackadaisical or too informal
8. Let themselves be taken advantage of.
9. Makes excuses
10. Non-assertive
11. Oversensitive emotionally
12. Possessive
13. Procrastinate
14. Easily manipulated
15. Shy
16. Slow or resistant to rushing, to change
17. Tearful, emotional
18. Wallow in self-pity
19. Whiner, complainer
20. Noncompetitive

Top Things to Do for an S

1. Acknowledge feelings
2. Appreciate and thank them for their work and efforts, gifts of appreciation
3. Ask them to join the group
4. Encourage them to be more decisive, self-confident and assertive
5. Give feedback with the sandwich approach (great work; needs improvement; great work)
6. Help them understand the importance of deadlines
7. Make them feel valuable and valued
8. Offer them plenty of time to finish projects
9. Prepare them for change
10. Provide a harmonious environment

Top Things Not to Do with an S

1. Abruptly change a project, timeline or routine
2. Allow them to become too clingy or dependent
3. Ask them to speed up or hurry
4. Ask them to step up in any role without lots of lead time and planning
5. Be embarrassed by their helpfulness and gift-giving
6. Be unappreciative of support, assistance or participation
7. Belittle anyone's feelings or contribution
8. Belittle their attachment to family and close friends
9. Don't gossip about or criticize others in front of them
10. Expect them to be confident and assertive in an unknown environment
11. Expect them to work alone
12. Expect them to work without a plan or clear step-by-step instructions
13. Let deadlines slide by unmet
14. Let them get sucked in to someone's problems, or taken advantage of by others
15. Let them procrastinate about starting any task
16. Let them whine or have a 'pity-party'
17. Publicly reprimand, criticize or shout at them
18. Surprise them with change
19. Take them for granted
20. Tell them their help is not needed

S's Fears

- Aggressiveness
- Being shunned
- Conflict
- Loss of security

Top Tips for an S's Growth

If you are the strong **S,** beware that your trusting nature doesn't come across as naïveté, because that is when others will take advantage of you. Your natural patience with people leads them to walking all over you, disrespecting you, stressing you out— instead, just nip it in the bud and change the subject . . . walk away . . . or just say 'No.'

Don't let your relaxed, steady **S**-speed communicate laziness or complacency—especially to the high-speed **D** or **I** managing or depending on you.

You do not overreact when someone shouts at you, pushes you, or just talks at you all the time—rather just remember that others may be less emotional than you or less sensitive to your feelings, quite unintentionally.

Their natural people orientation takes **S**'s away from task focus. Therefore, any **S** individual on the job must learn how to plan the work to be done—and then to work according to that plan.

Practice doing tasks faster, so that you can do them more quickly when the need arises (for instance, for the team's effectiveness or to meet a new deadline).

Show up, prepared and on time—but also prepared to do more on your own (independently) without the support of a team. Remember how capable you are!

Don't let differences distress you. Stop being overly sensitive—not everyone is out to hurt your feelings; they may be less sensitive to feelings than you are and oblivious to your values or your point of view. Remember: Not Everyone Is Like You . . . or will like you. And that is just fine!

You help others willingly, now learn to ask for help when you need it . . . and don't be so picky or hard to please about what you are offered.

Be yourself, and others will like you just fine—you don't need to give gifts to people or do things for them in order to earn their approval, respect and friendship.

Be more assertive. It is quite natural that not everyone will agree with you or you with them, so do not be so quick to withdraw, feel hurt, get whiny or teary. No one on the planet agrees with everyone about everything. That means you don't need to, either. Stand your ground for your values and believe in your value to others.

Don't be afraid of ruffling others' feathers. Many people may have less patience than you for lots of chit chat—including your apologies, excuses or long-winded explanations—so try to get to the point quickly (with just the facts) with those types of individuals and groups.

Phrases to Use That Encourage S's Energy

None of these energizing and encouraging phrases will surprise you now that you know the S style:

- "We really, really need your help!"
- "This is an important event for us, so we thought of you. There is plenty of time to plan and prepare, and we already have that detailed checklist from last year that you can use. It's all clearly mapped out."
- "We have just the team for you."
- "Mary needs to talk this through with someone, and you are such a good listener. Can I send her in?"
- "I'm so grateful that you were patient with my son last week."
- "Thanks so much—we have really appreciated your support! It has meant the world to us."

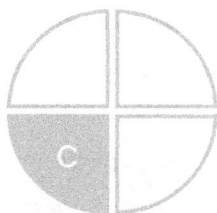

Chapter 8

Position Yourself
in the Bigger Pattern:
The 'C'

AT THIS point, we have studied the 'pure' or 'strong' forms of the **D** style (for dominance), the **I** style (for influence), and the **S** style (for steadiness).

    C is the fourth of our four behavioral styles and stands for *Conscientiousness*.

 **A Word of Caution**

    Please recall that I am again presenting a *nonexistent* individual displaying a very strong **C** style of behaviors and only those. I believe each of us can recognize ourselves in some

196 | BEHAVE! (AND WHY WE ALWAYS DO)

of the descriptions of these **C** behaviors. That is because each of us has created our own recipe of **D, I, S,** and **C** tendencies and patterns and made it our very own.

Also keep in mind that even if an individual is indeed a strong **C** as his single dominant style, that individual will not possess each and every one of the characteristics I'm presenting here. An individual can have a strong **C** style with only a handful of these behaviors.

Where Are These C People?

According to the reference I am using, strong **C's** make up 20-25% of the population. And we need every one of them because they are the ones who want to 'get it right' for the rest of us!

This is the fourth of our four major behavioral styles, and just as I know that you have strong **D, I** and **S** individuals around you, I can almost guarantee that you also have one or two strong **C's**.

As you read about the strong **C** in these pages, and if you are a parent, you may start to understand some of the apparently 'obsessive' behaviors of one of your children. If you are a team leader on the job, you might just start to understand which type of worker (in terms of behavioral styles) your team is missing and desperately needs for its success.

I cannot reiterate enough that if you employ or supervise individuals in the workplace, deal with raising or guiding children (such as running a daycare facility or counseling children, in addition to having your own children at home), the benefits of understanding all four of these behavioral styles (and your personal style) are priceless to you. These pure styles, which form the basis of the combination styles (some of which I will present in the next chapter), firstly open your awareness to what your own expectations and behaviors are in interactions with other individuals. Secondly, you start to see how simple it is to understand other people's behaviors in order to create harmony in work teams or in the home, or to gently adapt your own behavior as needed to create the productive or harmonious outcomes you prefer in your own environment.

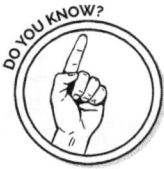

The 'C'—Do You Know Anyone Like This?

As I present the pure **C** style and describe the patterns of all strong **C** individuals, again, do two things for yourself. The first is to see if you recognize yourself in any of the descriptions I give about the **C's** behavioral style—even if it's only one tendency. Second, see if anyone you know in your family, at your workplace, in the community you are involved in presents any of these behaviors. As you watch television or go to the movies, also try to discern the strong **C** behaviors of celebrities and public figures, or of characters in films.

It has recently occurred to me that famous novelists, classic storytellers, and even originators of our traditional fairy tales probably had at least an intuitive understanding of each of these four behavioral styles. If you read character development in a novel that makes no sense to you, perhaps that writer has no idea about behavior patterns. On the other hand, a great number of novelists are good at building convincing characters that you will recognize as very strong **D's**, strong **I's**, strong **S's** or strong **C's**. Use film, storytelling, observation on television of celebrities and public figures, and your fiction reading to sharpen your ability to recognize these four behavior patterns. They are, without a doubt, all around you!

Andrei is a strong **C** who today is a young man in a promising career. Let's look at Andrei's earlier years.

> From the earliest years, Andrei was a model student. He was interested in school, and prepared for it every morning with attention to his personal grooming, always wearing neat and clean clothing which he fussed over a bit the night before.
>
> Some of the boys at school noticed that he hated to get messy or dirty, and would lead him into circumstances where that would happen. Andrei would then spend a grumpy quarter hour in the lavatory cleaning up as best he could; he'd spend the rest of the day trying to be invisible.
>
> Despite this type of teasing, his strength at studying and preparing for tests drew other students to him for help.

He was nervous and shy about doing that and tried to send them away, but kids are kids and they eventually cajoled him into helping them. Thus, shy as he was, he was drawn in and made friends.

How do we go about most easily recognizing a strong **C** style individual? And it is pretty easy. Simply look for someone who stays in the shadows of the sidelines, and is so reserved that he or she will never speak unless spoken to. This is a person who seems desperate to get away from the crowd. Walk through your offices, and whichever individuals it is virtually impossible to pull away from their deep concentration on the task at hand might just be your strong **C**'s. **C**'s are highly organized and neat as a pin, not only in their work spaces, but in their personal living spaces and of their person.

Memory Jogging Words for the Conscientious C—Is This You?

Let's use our trick of using memory-jogging words that begin with the letter **C** for this behavioral style. **C**'s are much more than what these words alone may be able to illustrate, but it is a good way to get used to the style. Remember that the **DISC** descriptive word for the **C** style is **conscientiousness.**

Conscientious, competent, cautious, careful, correct, calculator, critical thinker, compliant, correctness, completeness, conformity, compliant, control, conviction, consistent, cognitive, concerned

These are the people that say, "Seeing is believing—so show me—prove it to me!"

We need to **convince** them. So we could say that C stands for **convince!** Conversely, however, the C loves to be **correct**, accurate, and of all the four styles they know what "do your homework" really means. They become so sure that they are **correct** that there is no changing their mind. The person who coined the phrase, "He who is convinced against his will is of the same opinion still" was probably staring down a stubborn C when he said it. The C is not stubbornly of his opinion because of pride or because he believes he's better than anyone else. He just enjoys being right . . .

The strong C is very rarely 'only' **competent**. What I mean is that the strong C's love of detail, desire for **correctness** and search for **complete** answers is a strong push to doing deep research, **calculating** and studying to make a provable, airtight case every time. That all synergistically works together to (quite often) make the C an *expert* in the field.

Strong C's are quite **conscientious** about everything they undertake. They have an ability to tune out distractions in order to focus completely, with 100% of their **cognitive** and **critical** thinking abilities, to **complete** a task. This said, they can get lost in the details and lose track of the project's deadline, because they want to get all the details just right.

Strong **C**'s demand **compliance** of themselves and of others. In their mind, it's very easy to simply follow instructions as written (they wonder, "Why wouldn't we?"), or to do what they're supposed to do by law, or to stick to an agreement they have signed. They have strong **convictions** about doing the right thing, and doing it in the **correct** and **compliant** way. In this sense, they also show their **conformity;** they stay with what is low-risk, expected and well-known.

If you're dealing with a **complicated** or **complex** situation, problem, or formula—or faced with a business deal in which something doesn't seem quite right—go to the **C** for his **critical thinking capabilities**. The strong **C** can get to the bottom of it with uncanny ability.

The strong **C** is quite a **cautious** individual. No high-risk ventures for him! Because of the **caution**, along with the **C**'s natural eye to **correctness** and **completeness**, the **C**'s might need some help with time management. They don't like to be hurried in their thrust to get everything just so, and they tend to act like the need for a deadline is less important than the need for **correctness** and **care**.

· ·

QUICK QUIZ: Can you go back into the story of Andrei, above, and underscore the descriptive words and phrases that show how he is behaving from a purely **C** style?

· ·

Keep Up with the C

You won't need your jogging shoes to keep pace with the strong **C**! A slow to moderate pace of activities suits you strong **C's** best, with plenty of lead time to get things done right (by your self-imposed high standards). A pure **C** could sit at a desk for a whole day without thinking to get up for a break or change of pace when engrossed in a project. That means that other, faster-paced behavioral styles will have to dial back their impatience with you—indeed, they'll want to urge you to keep up with them, rather than slow down to match your pace.

Are C's Thing or People Oriented?

You **C's** are quite shy, reserved and quiet around people, and that is why your comfort zone is with tasks and things. You are a task-oriented person. You excel at getting tasks done that require undistracted focus and analytical attention, and you do them well . . . at your own slow and meticulous sort of pace.

If you are first seeing a strong **C** in a group environment . . . he is the one you don't see! The **C's** shy away from crowds, are not social (sometimes are even anti-social) or chatty. Getting them to speak is 'like pulling teeth.'

Research—which is absolutely task-oriented behavior—is one of the **C's** great loves and strengths. It is the way a **C** proves that he is right, that his recommendations will work, that his analyses are correct. It also is solo work and keeps him away from groups, which he likes.

Let's have another look at Andrei in his youth.

> Andrei flew through school, excelling in science, math, logic, and got high marks on all essay papers requiring the demonstration that he had done lots of research. He was drawn to studying forensic biology at the University level, but after two years moved over to the area of forensic accounting. Lately, Andrei has been considering adding the law to his list of degrees. He is considering going full-time days as versus night classes only. He is still weighing the advantages and the disadvantages of each solution.

You Might Be a C If . . .

Keep in mind that you won't find any individual out in the world who is solely of these **C** tendencies, styles, motivations and characteristics. This is just my way of laying it on thick enough that you grasp the heart and soul of what the **C** behavioral style really is, so that you recognize it in a wink. You have probably already identified a few of these behaviors in people you know who are not pure **C**'s. We'll get to that in the next chapter.

If you have been reading attentively, (which by the way is a strong **C** trait), you will have already identified in your personal behaviors some of the **D**, some of the **I**, and some of the **S** traits, tendencies, motivations, strengths and weaknesses. That is totally normal!

Let's add some layers now to the strong **C** behavior style to round out not only this style, but all four **DISC** behavioral patterns.

A Snapshot of the C Style

The C-style individual is a "glass half empty" or pessimistic type of individual, with little to no sense of humor. You **C's** have a tendency to point out problems before they exist.

The strong **C** is the most analytical and detail oriented of our four styles. They will often be overly analytical and perfectionist, and are self-critical when they personally feel they are not doing an exact enough job. When pushed by another behavior style's tendency to sloppiness or generalities, the strong **C** will become quite critical of their work product or process.

C's can focus to the exclusion of all distractions around them for hours and hours—pouring over facts, data, information, relevant reference sources and proven resource materials.

Although they are not always overtly antisocial, they are the least social and most reserved and private of the four behavioral styles, and are quite happy working alone, and left alone to their own devices. Don't demand that a strong **C** show up at a social event, or a business event where he is expected to mingle and network. Though the strong **C** might do it out of a sense of duty or obligation, he will be very stiff and closemouthed and tremendously uncomfortable.

Their biggest fear is that their work will be criticized. And they do not take criticism very well when it comes to their beloved work ethic. Their goal is to make sure everything works the way it should, according to the rules and regulations and the instructions set forth before they began the job. They want to make it right, exact, perfect. If it is pointed out that they have not achieved that goal, they will become quite defensive. They are logical thinkers, systematic workers, cautious and low- to no-risk takers, very methodical.

Under pressure, the C becomes overly critical and overly focused on problems that are tiny details—that may be seen by those on the receiving end as nitpicky. If they become critical of others when under pressure, understand that they are always very self-critical, and demand perfection and perfect work from themselves. When stressed, they demand more of themselves.

They may seem like slow pokes, and compared to other behavioral styles they prefer a slow to moderate pace for doing anything. This said, they would rather be given time to do anything right the first time, than to have to take time to do it over again later. They don't work well when deadlines are moved up in the middle of a project, nor do they appreciate short timelines for what they perceive as complex, research intensive work.

They prefer written communication and instructions. When that written communiqué originates with them, they will load it with facts and details—the strong C writes the longest memos of any other style.

Because they are not people oriented, they will not express an opinion willingly or spontaneously. The best way to find out what's on their mind, or to have them share their knowledge and expertise or their findings, is to ask them specifically for that information. And then, they only speak when they feel they know the subject matter very well.

Because the strong **C** loves research and answering the question 'why?' that invariably comes to mind during research, these individuals often develop intimate, detailed knowledge of a subject, and are often lauded as experts in their field.

Strong **C's** want to know the reason behind everything they undertake, including school homework projects, work projects and family affairs. You **C's** can be heard repeatedly asking your favorite question, "Why?" "Why is this necessary?" "Why is this true?" as some of your most pressing questions!

C's are focused on making correct decisions and avoiding mistakes; this often results in great decision-making, but also in *slow* decision-making. When under pressure, the **C's** tendency to collect more information, data, and details is exacerbated and makes them even slower in deciding than ever.

Success for the **C** comes from an ability to systematically focus their efforts on the task at hand; from not being easily distracted from a goal; from demanding high-quality work; from being very structured and industrious. When in-depth planning is what makes for a successful outcome, call on the **C. C's** are finishers—every time. They are well prepared, love collecting knowledge, facts and data, and can become very much a subject matter expert or highly skilled in a given technique or field—and are often recognized as The Expert.

Failure comes to the **C** when he is so set on getting the details right that he criticizes every little, tiny wrong one, or when she is so set on getting everything 'more' perfect, that she misses vital deadlines. They are such pre-project planners, foreseeing every last detail and need, that they can be perceived as non-starters or slow starters on assigned work, rather than a quick self-starter.

You strong **C's** are cautious, the most reserved of the four styles, and quite private. **C's** prefer a formal approach in all interactions, and often never speak up unless asked a specific question.

In all you undertake, pure **C's** value being seen as accurate, trustworthy and dependable. You are clear thinkers, and others can depend upon you to see details they might have missed. You need lots of time to plan ahead. You need time because you will consider all facts, information, data and numbers that are available about the situation.

As much as you fear having your work criticized, you like praise when it is well-done. However, not in public! You really want to be right and worked well to achieve that, and appreciate quiet, private recognition of your accuracy and the quality of your work. Something in writing is just fine with you.

New teams of people for every project you work on are not your thing. Although you prefer by far to work alone on any project or task, you readily agree to work with a select few others—the same people over and over again, as much as possible—that you already know and feel comfortable with.

Key Spoken Words and Phrases of the C Style

Strong **C** individuals are usually very diplomatic and polite—sometimes even too polite and too conventional or reserved in their choice of words. Because they are the most introverted of the **DISC** styles, they tend to share only a minimal amount of information that they deem is necessary to the conversation, often speaking in short, choppy-sounding sentences. Their shyness makes them self-conscious about what they say and how, so listeners may get the impression that the strong **C** is weighing every word (and they are).

Their conversations are very rarely of a personal nature, and they won't be seeking you out for a little bit of informal or personalized chitchat anytime soon. However, when they are presenting a report, findings of some of their work, any kind of technical data or proofs of their research, they may just drown you in a talkative ocean of technical terms and jargon, numbers and all sorts of data, and in-depth detailed descriptions that lose you from the start. All presented in their slow, even speaking voice . . .

As you can guess, the **C**'s are pretty quiet people, and are loners (and like it that way). They will not readily enter a conversation, but will participate when asked specific questions or for an opinion on a clear topic. You **C**'s are liable to respond to requests for help or work assignments with something like:

- "I hope I'll be able to meet everyone's high expectations."
- "Measure twice, cut once."
- "But I hope there is plenty of time for me to perform all the research involved?"
- "I won't let you down, because I'm going to consider this problem from all angles."
- "Do we have enough time to do it all accurately and correctly?"

You also might hear a strong **C** individual say things such as:

- "Let me get all our ducks in a row before we jump in to this project."
- "The devil is in the details."
- "We have to do it right the first time."
- "If we don't have time to do it the right the first time, how will we ever find the time to do it over again?"

Others say about the strong **C**:

- "She is the perfect hostess; she'd really thought of everything for that event."
- "Our child is a technically disciplined student; we just wish he'd let go and be more creative and spontaneous."
- "Boy, he drives me crazy! His routine is so rigid and he expects me to follow it. I can set my watch by his procedures."

- "Good thing she has an assistant. She gets so absorbed in the calculations she's been doing, that she rarely even hears her phone ring."
- "He wouldn't have said a word if I hadn't asked him to speak up about it. Good grief, the whole deal might have gone down the toilet without his research saving the day!"

Key Body Language of the C Style

C's prefer formality and it shows in their highly-controlled body language. The C may come across as unemotional, standoffish, formal or distant, even wooden in his movements or lack thereof. Strong C's are the hardest of the four styles to get to know on a personal basis.

Their faces are often glued into a neutral position. They won't smile or laugh at the usual jokes or express any appreciation of your humorous stories—but that doesn't mean they don't need your kindness, or that they dislike you. It's just their strong C style in play.

The strong C, whether child or adult, is fastidious about his appearance and will avoid looking messy or dirty or shabby. Clothing is classic and conservative, in cut and color; C's wear polished shoes. Their grooming is impeccable with manicured hands and neat hair. In the extreme, this fastidiousness can push C's to changing clothes several times a day, redoing makeup, etc.

In social circumstances (personal or business gatherings), it is the C who appears physically poised and polished—when you can get him there in the first place. He maintains good eye contact without staring. His handshake is firm and brief. The **C** is the most reserved and withdrawn of all the styles, and will often be found sitting against a wall if required to be at a large event such as a party.

The **C** displays impeccable, respectful manners and will, for instance, wait to be invited before sitting or before entering a room or before joining a group whose conversation is in progress.

Because the **C** is so focused and able to tune out distractions, **C's** can sit for hours without getting up or exercising.

This said, when the **C** is an athlete in training, they are extremely disciplined and actually enjoy the routine of daily practice and workouts, and the tedium of repetition required to perfect their skills. This is because of their ability to not focus so much on the tedium and routine, but on the real goal of perfecting all the tiny details that are part of their athletic skill set. They're good at analyzing and planning strategies to improve team plays, or to improve their own body's efficient movement in solo sports.

Demotivating, Discouraging and Distressing the C

The **C** is not comfortable getting to know new people. Don't throw the strong **C** into a different team for every new task to be done, or expect them to network and mingle at business events!

Our friends of the **C** style are discouraged, demotivated or depressed by:

→ Continually *changing* rules, policies, 'standard' operating procedures, performance expectations, levels of acceptable quality

→ Short time to process information, amass and analyze details, compile detailed reports

→ Required socializing

→ Constantly changing team composition

→ No, or inconsistent, quality control

→ Criticism of their work processes or end product of their work efforts

→ Situations in which high emotions play a role

→ Being asked for personal information

What Motivates or Stimulates the C?

The strong **C** is motivated by excellence, complete and provable answers, value. The **C's** get excited when tasks require concision and exactness, detailed pre-project planning and carrying out the plan. Hearing "We have a new project, and here is how your particular skill set can help get it done right." is really exciting for you.

Our friends of the **C** style are enthused and motivated by:

→ Being right, and being able to prove that they are to others

→ Logical, systematic and organized approaches to any task or problem

→ Being rewarded for high quality, correctness, and precision work

→ Specific appreciative feedback that validates their work process or work results

→ Seeing that they are given plenty of time to do a high-quality job

→ No-nonsense, businesslike environments with task orientation and high-quality expectations

Let's check in on Andrei in present time, on the job.

He got his international public auditor certifications in the first round of testing (which is usually pretty hard to achieve), and is currently working as a forensic auditor—an accountancy specialization looking for evidence of fraud in money handling.

In fact, Andrei has been hired by the Board of Directors of a corporation to head a team of forensic accountants and auditors on a project basis. They have set forth their concerns to him, for which they at present have no proof, of monies being irregularly transferred to overseas businesses and back again. Andrei's team is charged with examining the money trail and determining if anything illegal or unethical is taking place—and proving it with hard-and-fast documentary evidence if there is.

One fellow on the Board of Directors, interestingly, understands **DISC** behavior styles, and he took a wild guess at Andrei's preferred behavior style being the strong **C** . . . not to mention most of his team members'. He thus made sure the Directors set a comfortable deadline for him to present his first findings, and granted him full access to all the resources and company people that he would need.

Talents and Careers of the C

The **C** is a natural planner who is focused on quality. The strong **C** is analytical, organized and structured, logical and detail-oriented. If you want something done right the first time, give the job to a **C**—they will do the research, plan out the job and structure the steps of the task, and keep a close eye on all the details involved. They are finishers.

You **C's** are all about the details, step-by-step processes and rules, accuracy, and high standards. You're all about process and systems. As such, you are a detail-focused analyst able to weigh the pros and cons for management or for a decision-making team. Working from logic, process and systems is what you like best. You hate when rules, processes, or scope of work change constantly or with little notice.

The strong **C's** are great at playing the devil's advocate on any project, in their department, or for any team. The **C** will make sure that there is a repeatable process (or several of them) in place, providing consistent outcomes, if they have anything to say about things.

If you just can't afford to make any mistakes, hire a strong **C** employee—like that Board of Directors did by hiring Andrei.

Careers which might suit a strong **C** style:

→ Judge
→ Litigation attorney; litigation paralegal (presenting complex, research- and investigation-rich cases in the courts of law)
→ Surgeon
→ Engineer
→ Editor
→ Quality control auditor or inspector
→ Researcher
→ Accountant; comptroller; auditor
→ Investigator
→ Programmer or data processor
→ Financial officer
→ City planner
→ Efficiency expert
→ Statistician
→ Software developer
→ Computer technician (building or repairing)
→ Tax preparer

C's are great on jobs where you need detailed accuracy, top-quality end product, or to prove your points in logical, analytical ways. C's are good choices on jobs when you need someone who will meet exact requirements, find and correct errors, document references and resources. Strong C's are the right person to choose when you have tedious work that needs to be done by a single individual over long hours at a stretch.

Do's and Don'ts for C 's

Like the other behavioral styles we've discussed, the strong C's have a blind spot about themselves.

Non-C individuals almost immediately notice that the strong C puts high expectations and standards of quality, completeness, proof and accuracy as their top priority, yet strong C's do not see themselves that way at all. As you have read this chapter, though, you see that these characteristics are the core, the heart and soul, of a strong C behavior style!

Do This

Be aware the C's need structure and time to plan before starting a project.

Express specific appreciation of their logical or critical thinking in front of others, and give critical feedback in private.

Gently insist that the **C** listens to and fully considers your and others' opinions and needs within the framework of the task. You might get him listening if you say that it is his "research into options that exist elsewhere!"

Understand the **C**'s need for privacy, to work alone as often as is feasible for your team or your business, and to take their time.

Gently insist that the **C** backs off their demands on others for perfection in every detail. This is where you might try to help the **C** individual appreciate the benefits of compromise. Call to their attention that they are the ones who are great at detail, accuracy and logical analysis—but not to expect others to be as gifted at it as they are.

Try to hear out **C**'s logical analyses first, remembering that the **C**'s preference is low or no risk, which just might protect you and your interests in the end.

Go to a **C** when you need exacting, rigorous research or due diligence. Consult a **C** when something feels off—about a person, a circumstance, a report, a business deal, or analysis someone else has produced—and give the **C** the resources and time to find out what is wrong.

Don't Do This

Don't expect emotional or humorous arguments to win over the **C**. Also, don't expect a strong **C** to spontaneously stand and share his opinion, findings or present contradictory proofs without being asked.

Do not publicly contradict or criticize the **C** or his work. Take it private and make it specific.

Never try to rush a **C** into giving you a quick result or fast decision—that is paramount to trashing his work, his process and preparation, his skills.

Do stand your ground before a perfection-seeking, overly demanding **C** and do not allow the **C** to set *your* standards of excellence. Don't feel intimidated by or inferior as measured against the expectations of a boss who is a strong **C**.

Don't wave off the importance of details in front of a **C**. He simply won't believe you! As all **C's** know and believe, "The devil is in the details." To a **C**, ignoring details is tantamount to inviting failure. Even the easiest project depends on the success of the smallest components, according to a strong **C**.

Key Strengths of the C

As I have said about each of these behavior styles, we need each of them. It's this variety that makes the world go 'round! It's this variety that gets things done in our families and in our organizations.

The strong **C** has some terrific strengths, which are intellectual analysis, mental concentration and focus, and logic. The strong **C** individuals are great planners and organizers. They are industrious and tenacious. They have a strong sense of compliance (adherence) to rules, obedience to laws and to what is the right thing.

One of their natural tendencies is to pre-plan well enough such that a task is done correctly and completely the first time. If your team is made up only of other non-C individuals, call on the C to do the planning.

Although it may not seem like a strength to other behavior styles, the strong C can take monotony, rote work, clear lists of instructions in his stride. Think of times when you need someone who can just sit down and stay with it until it is done, or who can just follow instructions as written, and you'll find a strong C!

As I've said elsewhere, each of these four styles can find their place in a leadership role. As just one example of when a strong C would be your ideal leader for a team, think of circumstances where you have hostile, maverick or out of control individuals (or even the entire team, which needs a firm hand to not only maintain order, but to provide a strong sense of knowing what to do). The C style leaders can motivate others to perfect their skills and raise their levels of competency or efficiency. They can keep teams and individuals in the team disciplined and focused on the shared goal and its achievement with great excellence. As coaches (and not only in sports), their ability to plan and practice their team all the way to victory is well-appreciated at the end of the day.

The C's have a natural focus (some people see it as narrow-mindedness), and desire that everything be correct and precise (others see it as argumentativeness). How can that all be a strength? It can help you avoid many a hazardous or unsafe situation, piece of equipment or decision. It can help you get better terms in a negotiation. It can simply shame other non-C individuals to perform at a higher standard or with more efficiency or precision!

Weaknesses of the C Behavior Style

The very strong **C** individuals, if they feel pressure or that they are losing control over any task, can ratchet up their natural perfectionism into an obsession, ratchet up their cautiousness into stubbornness and zero risk-taking.

Their attachment to high standards and excellence can go to such extremes that people on **C's** team simply give up in frustration or revolt, because they cannot perform to the strong **C's** high expectations and demands for perfection.

As we have seen, the **C** is highly self-critical, and when that behavior is ratcheted up, it turns into unpleasant criticism of others, and even sarcasm of their capabilities and abilities.

The **C's** are naturally slow-paced individuals who are pessimistic and cautious. How is this a weakness? If they are the only **C** on a team, it can drive the other non-**C** style people crazy!

Strong **C's** argue over tiny details and trivialities, and when hearing your exaggerations might even consider them to be lies. If an authority figure, such as a professor or other teacher, seems to have made an error in any statement or presentation—you can be sure it will be a strong **C** in the classroom who points it out.

They become anxious or irritated when others don't follow policy, the law, rules or instructions. Likewise, the **C** is the one in the room who gets upset when discussions move off topic.

Are C's Extremes Good or Bad?

The 'opposite' behavior style for the strong **C** is the strong **I**. The strong **I's** faster pace and nonstop talking repels the strong **C** and pushes him out of the room. **C's** may be suspicious of the **I's** enthusiasm, asking themselves 'Why?' and wondering what there is to be so gushingly enthusiastic about. Frankly, it embarrasses the **C**!

Like all the other behavioral styles, the **C** can seem over-the-top to us, overly-reactive or extreme when any of his behaviors are not what we expect. But let me remind you of this—all of us, whatever our behavioral style, have our own comfort zone and sense of being in or out of control.

When we are pushed out of our natural comfort zone or feel like we are losing control, we do what we can to regain control and to move back into our preferred environment. This is when our usual behaviors might seem extreme to others. Good or bad? Right or wrong? Behavioral styles depend on *context*. Your interpretation of context is not the same as another person's. As you come to better understand all four of these **DISC** styles of behavior, you can step back and let the other individual work through his discomfort, or use some of the tips in each chapter (the do's and don'ts) to help him move more quickly back into a feeling of 'normalcy.'

C's Extremes

Have you ever heard of *"analysis paralysis?"* That would be one of the most frustrating extremes (in the other **DISC** styles' viewpoint) of the extreme **C**! That is an extreme version of the **C's** outstanding strength and ability to organize details and to analyze patterns—which many company owners and managers would agree is a valuable skill in the workplace.

Likewise, asking Why? too often—for instance by repeatedly questioning current processes or ways of doing things, ostensibly to ensure that things are done correctly, accurately and perfectly—can turn the systematic and efficient **C's** to irritating 'whyners' (in the opinion of the other **DISC** styles).

The strong **C** is typically quality- and detail-focused. However, when they ratchet their typical or usual behaviors into their extreme versions, that can push those two qualities into perfectionism, a demanding obsession to get it right and an obsession for details and even more details.

Now that you have understood a bit better the **C** behavior style, look at the following extreme behaviors and see if you can name the usual behavior they stem from.

→ Humorlessness

→ Inflexibility

→ Narrow-minded

→ Paralysis

→ Stubborn and unrelenting

→ Tunnel vision

The C—Is This Someone You Interact with?

Look around you. If you know anyone in your family or on your team whose greatest strength is planning in detail, getting things right or whose predominant aptitude is logical analysis and critical thinking—you are interacting with a strong **C** style individual. If you notice someone who is annoyed (or worse!) by *inaccuracy* and *incorrectness* or *lack* of detail—likewise, you are interacting with a strong **C**. If you are observing a family or team member and notice how serious they are, and that their tendency is to sit on the sidelines on their own, that too might be a strong **C** individual.

Now that you have information that others may not about behavior patterns, try to come up with some approaches to not only get along very well with the strong **C** (assuming that you are not that **C**), but to help others interact harmoniously with the strong **C's** around them.

Interacting Successfully with the C

The **C** will respond best to a supervisor or team leader who is reassuring, has an open-door policy and like the **C**, appreciates a detail-orientation, and concise, clearly-defined operating standards.

The strong **C** needs clearly defined tasks and explanations, with sufficient time and resources to accomplish them. Although the strong **C** is a loner by preference, participating in a team is acceptable if the team members are known and familiar.

To motivate the strong **C** on the job, consider assigning that individual the research for the team's projects, and instead of asking them to present orally in front of a group, ask them to present their findings in written form. Make sure you tell the **C** the maximum number of pages that report may take (otherwise the **C** will give you much more than you expect, need, or could ever read).

In the home, that might call for asking your **C** child to google/ research all the details of an excursion that you are planning as a family, or to research the top three items for a home purchase you want to make. This allows the **C** to collect information and data, and answer their recurring question—Why?

When assigning research for work, school, volunteerism or family needs, be sure to circumscribe the task quite clearly in its scope and in its deadline. Otherwise, the **C** will go far beyond what you expected. It will all be quality work, but probably overwhelming (especially to non-**C**'s) in its detail.

When you are communicating with strong **C**'s, just avoid the small talk and personal questions, and get down to business right away. Be sure to provide them with specific facts they need from you, and explain the logic behind the decisions you have made. As the strong **C**'s are always organized and prepared, so should you be once you draw them in to any discussion or meeting that involves them. Remembering that the strong **C** tends to be a slow-moving, steady-paced individual—and that applies to time they need to think things through and respond to you—give them plenty of time to think over what has been presented to them or to ask you their questions. They are not 'slow' thinkers at all, nor are they slow to understand you. It is just that they are silently turning over great amounts of data and information in their head before responding or asking you anything. And it's no surprise that their numerous questions will be about the details! They will appreciate it when you say you don't know, but can find out, or that you don't know, but so-and-so can give them the answer.

In public or in private, the **C's** in your organization or family don't handle criticism well at all. Expect defensiveness! Since their overriding thrust is to be correct in all their work (and they may not be), you'll need to be firm but gentle in showing them what you need. Say, for instance, "This is great work. I think you may need to double check this one area—just for my own comfort, based on what I've heard in the past. Would you mind?" They'll indeed go back to their resources and references, double check so they can prove you wrong (and discover, perhaps, that they were). They're happy to do it, because in the end, their work is perfectly correct . . . and they'll always aim for perfection.

What If I Am Not All This One Style?

I trust that you have a clear picture in your mind of the 'pure' or strong **C** style at this point. You have probably (I would be shocked if it were not the case) recognized at least one **C** trait in your own behaviors . . . as well as one or more in each of the **D, I, S** styles.

I suggest that you review all your notes about the **D, I, S** and **C** styles that describe **_you_**. Can you decide from your notes which of the four styles is your predominant or strongest style? You might be torn between two styles that seem equally strong. You are probably certain which style is your least important one. Just play with it for a few minutes, then go on to the next chapter where I will illustrate how these four styles become entwined. We look at samplings in chapter 9 of how these four patterns can double up and create a nuanced, richer, more unique personal style for you.

For now, let's wrap up the strong **C** style.

Just for Fun

→ Favorite question: Why?
→ Favorite color: Yellow
→ Preferred animal: Tropical fish
→ Favorite car: Toyota; Honda
→ Favorite mottos: "A stitch in time saves nine."
  "Let's do it right the first time."
→ Song: The Gambler
→ Life philosophy: "Don't show all your cards"
→ Preferred magazines: Consumer Reports; PC Magazine; DIY Pro (PC=personal computing; DIY=do it yourself)
→ Target: "Ready . . . Aim . . . Aim . . . Aim . . . "
→ Top three needs of a strong C: Correctness; quality; answers

In Summary

The strong **C** individual is the most-task oriented of our four styles. They prefer to work alone, and will generally only speak up in groups when asked for some specific information or his opinion on a particular issue.

Strong **C's** are probably the least people-oriented of our four styles; in fact, they are wallflowers. Don't ask them to network, mix, mingle or chitchat in groups. They don't know how to do it. They don't understand why you would even want them to. For the **C's**, "It's not personal, it's business." Give them a task to do, as long as it is not to do with people!

They prefer to act from a slow to moderate pace, and never rush. When given a task to do, or a project with a deadline, they will always prefer to have the instructions clearly stated in writing, and the announced deadline far into the future. These are individuals who need to take their time. They are, however, not procrastinators! They need the time they request to preplan any task or project in great detail. They further need time while working on the task to perform deep and often multifaceted research, or to do complex analyses, or 'run the numbers' numerous times for accuracy. As part of written instructions, a non-**C** supervisor or project leader or teacher is well advised to include the maximum length allowed for any written report or resultant research paper—otherwise you will be inundated with far more pages and details that you want.

These are fastidious, well-organized, neat planners, whose primary goal is to do anything they undertake correctly, completely and perfectly. These attributes leak over into all aspects of their life. They are neatly and conservatively dressed and well-groomed. **C's** are organized and orderly of their possessions, such that they often know to a millimeter if any of their things have been moved . . . and they will proceed to immediately move it back to their assigned space.

They are sticklers for following rules, regulations, established procedures and processes, and laws of the land. They simply cannot understand why anyone would color outside these boundaries to do anything that is 'not allowed.' They are happy with what the other **DISC** styles would call tedium, and can sit for hours without moving if they are on a job that requires their undivided focus. A stampede of elephants through the room wouldn't distract them. . . .

Like each of the other behavioral styles, the **C's** can be pushed out of their comfort zones or be made to feel that they have lost control. This is when the strong **C** will ratchet up his usual behaviors into extremes such as 'analysis paralysis' (rather than just collecting the needed details). This might be when the strong **C** asks for justifications and rationalizations from you, by repeatedly asking 'why, why, why'—until he is called a 'why-ner' and people start fleeing when he comes into the room. Likewise, if the strong **C** feels that he is under pressure or very stressed to perform, he will become obsessively and disagreeably demanding of the members of his team, and nitpick over truly unimportant details and other minutia that most of the other styles wouldn't have even noticed. Chances are, he will drive his team members crazy . . . or drive them away for good.

The strong **C** is typically unable to understand or respond to humor. They have a tunnel vision, and an unrelenting stubbornness about getting things right, and getting things right the first time. They turned defensive when criticized about their work or if there is the mere suggestion that they have not submitted a perfect job.

If you have a **C** in the family, he or she will feel more comfortable when details, research and analysis are respected—and he or she is asked do it for the family's needs. In today's digital world, even children can sit and google information, prices and details for a family excursion or other household need. Encourage them to share of themselves in this way.

If you have a **C** in your workplace, that individual can be a tremendous asset if you understand and use his behavioral preferences and specific skills in the right way—his way! It will always be beneficial to you as supervisor and to the team the **C** is involved with, to help all team members understand about all four behavior styles, and which styles they each possess.

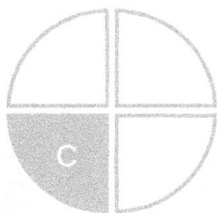

Chapter 8 bis

Charting the C Behavioral Style

C's Top Observable Characteristics

1. Asks why about everything
2. Attentive to the smallest details
3. Cautious in most things
4. Conservative
5. Critical
6. Formal in speech
7. Hates to be rushed
8. Humorless
9. Impeccably, but conservatively, groomed
10. Moderate pace in speech, takes a long time to respond to questions
11. Obsessive about having and keeping everything in the exact place they have assigned for it
12. Planner
13. Quiet until asked to specifically to speak
14. Regimented in daily routines
15. Reserved, tight body movement
16. Respect rules and procedures, laws and regulations
17. Subject matter expert
18. Unadorned office—functional only
19. Visible interest in technical, conceptual tasks and data
20. Withdrawn from conversations and groups

C's Typical Body and Verbal Language

- Asks, "Why?" about most things
- Formal and quiet speech
- Slow, tight, reserved body language, with little movement at all
- The wallflower, the loner

C's Top Motivators

1. Access to all data and facts for a task
2. Allotted plenty of time to plan in the detail
3. Appreciation of conscientiousness and work ethic
4. Appreciation of loyalty brought to the group, company, task
5. Asked for his thoughts, knowledge and opinion on technical and analytical issues
6. Being 'off the hook' when it comes to mingling in groups
7. Being left alone to do the task
8. Being recognized as expert
9. Being seen as the expert and consulted as such
10. Given complex or intricate tasks because "He's the expert"
11. Given detailed, logical written instructions for a project or free rein to create such a plan himself
12. Given lots of research to do
13. Giving and receiving the 'right answers,' accurate answers or facts
14. Left to organize things in preferred ways

15. Needing to deal in details
16. Plenty of time to perform accurately and complete the assignment
17. Routine rather than change
18. Someone else deals with interruptions
19. Specific rather than generic appreciation of his concision and perfectionism on a project or task
20. Thoroughly understanding the task at hand, the logic for doing it

C's Top Demotivators

1. Being asked to mingle or network in groups
2. Being assigned to a brand-new team of people over and over again
3. Being rushed to perform
4. People who swipe over the details or are happy with sloppy or incomplete work
5. People who don't respect expertise or details
6. Pressured into making quick decisions
7. Public criticism of his work
8. Short timelines for completion of 'correct' work
9. Working for a person who is dismissive of the importance of details
10. Working with others on any task

 **C's Top Strengths**

1. Analytical
2. Compliant to regulations and laws
3. Conscientious and industrial
4. Consistently produce high quality results
5. Detail-oriented
6. Follows rules and procedures
7. Great follow through
8. Great planners
9. Knowledgeable, often to the point of expertise
10. Loyal to their workplace
11. Organized
12. Patient with tedious tasks
13. Professional behavior
14. Reliable
15. Reliable finishers
16. Strong work ethic
17. Sustained focus
18. Systematic
19. Trustworthy
20. Welcomes complexity

C's Top Weaknesses

1. Accept criticism badly
2. Critical of others' poor work
3. Far too technical and detailed when speaking to most audiences
4. Hard to please
5. Humor-handicapped
6. Impatient, uncomfortable with people
7. Incapable of making small talk
8. Introverted
9. Loner
10. Obsessive
11. Overly analytical
12. Overly sensitive
13. Pessimistic—glass half-empty mindset
14. Poor or late starter, due for need to plan everything before beginning
15. Rigid
16. Shy
17. Slow, slow, slow
18. Socially uncomfortable, often to the point of being antisocial
19. Will not speak up or participate unless specifically asked
20. Withdrawn

C's Top Extremes

1. Defensive and lashes back when their work is questioned
2. Humorlessness
3. Inflexibility
4. Lash out in sharp criticism of others' work or participation in shared task
5. Narrow-minded
6. Paralysis, as in 'analysis-paralysis'
7. Stubborn and unrelenting
8. Social rigidity when pushed
9. Scornful of those not willing to rise to a high standard
10. Withdrawn and close-mouthed

Top Things to Do for an C

1. Allow him to work alone without micro-management
2. Appreciate and go to him for his skill with research and detail work
3. Ask specific questions and be patient with the **C's** need to think through the answers before speaking
4. Express specific appreciation for their work, and in front of others involved
5. Give critical feedback in private, with plenty of evidence supporting the critique
6. Give them a structure and plenty of time to plan
7. Remember their preference for low risk or no risk

8. Remind the **C** that others' participation and input may not be what he/she expects, but to evaluate it rationally nonetheless

9. Respect his reserve and need for privacy

10. Stand your ground before a perfection-seeking, overly-demanding **C**

Top Things Not to Do with an C

1. Allow the **C** to set *your* standards of excellence

2. Be funny or make jokes and expect a laugh

3. Be too sociable or chatty at any time

4. Bother them pointlessly during work time

5. Criticize a **C's** work without supporting evidence

6. Dismiss or ignore input when the **C** perceives self as expert

7. Expect a **C** to get along easily or comfortably with strangers

8. Expect a strong **C** to spontaneously chat and make light conversation

9. Expect emotional or humorous arguments to win over the **C**

10. Feel intimidated by or inferior to a strong **C**

11. Generalize

12. Get impatient with a **C** for wanting to take the time needed to 'get it right'

13. Get personal

14. Hold long brainstorming or indecisive meetings and expect **C** to stay calm

15. Make them appear inferior in their own field of endeavor

16. Make yourself look smarter

17. Nag them

18. Publicly contradict or criticize his work

19. Rush a **C** into giving you a quick result or fast decision

20. Wave off the importance of details

C's Fears

- Being in groups and expected to interact
- Change
- Criticism directed at him . . . about anything
- Rushing

Top Tips for a C's Growth

The **C** style has as many strengths as the other three styles, yet any strong **C** can identify areas in which he would like to improve. For the **C's** personal growth, the **C** might consider the following items.

Exercise your facial 'smile' muscle every once in a while. It doesn't hurt. It's possible to let go a bit in other ways too, for instance by letting go of your natural obsession with order, organization.

Understand that other people—non-**C's**—are intimidated by your demands for perfection into the detail. You don't have to give up quality of outcomes, but be more accepting of others' styles as they get you there. How can you express things so that people know your perfectionism is aimed at the task at hand, not at their personalities?

People might see you as quite indecisive, because they cannot hear the 'calculations' taking place in your head while they wait for you to speak or decide. Taking a calculated risk, and deciding (speaking out) more quickly, can be beneficial. In what types of situations could you allow yourself to calculate and decide more quickly without feeling 'impulsive' about it?

Respect leaders' needs to have work at the stated deadline. Deadlines must be met as part of the high standards of excellence that you pride yourself on—so work your plan, and don't get lost in the details. People depend on you providing your work on time, and as promised, so that they can then do their part of the project. *Try this* for better time management: Set your personal deadline one full day or two shorter than the mandated deadline. That gives you wiggle room to review your work or submission and be on time (or early!) for the team.

There are varying degrees of excellence and perfection—gray is a color along with black and white. Thorough explanations (those black-and-white answers) are not always possible in the workplace—or in life. Learn to work with the information provided. This is a type of compromise; doing tasks with others is often going to be about give-and-take. What approaches help you be more open to occasional compromise?

What will it take for you to see a 'glass half full' instead of a 'glass half empty'?

Phrases to Use That Encourage C's Energy

- "We need an analytical person, so I thought you'd be interested."
- "The details are beyond me. I know you're the expert, so can you help me make sense of them?"

- "They've written up the concept with some detail—it's all in the file—so can we count on you to tell us what's missing in the logic by, say, next week on Wednesday?"
- "You can do this on your own, right?"
- "How much time will you need?"
- "The big boss really appreciated your analysis and write-up, so I thought you'd want to know."

A Quiz
on Your Understanding

NOW THAT you have read the basics about the four pure **DISC** styles, let's test your knowledge. Answer the questions below according to the knowledge that you have just acquired. No pressure! Go back into the preceding chapters as needed.

1. The two styles that are fast-paced: _____ _____

2. Which of those fast-paced styles is so fast, we might call it a 'whirlwind' pace? _____

3. Name the two styles that are people-oriented: _____ _____

4. Of those styles, which one is more likely to invest in long-term relationship development? _____

continued...

5. As described, which style is the most:

_____Quiet and reserved, even a loner

_____Talkative and gregarious

_____Emotional (at least visibly)

_____'Get it done' oriented

6. Can you give 4 or more 'memory jogging words'

(words starting in the letter **D** for the Dominance style, etc.)

for the **D, I, S** and **C** styles?

D: _____, _____, _____, _____,

I: _____, _____, _____, _____,

S: _____, _____, _____, _____,

C: _____, _____, _____, _____,

7. Can you name the two styles that are happy to follow

rules and procedures, processes and instructions?

_____ _____

8. Which are the two styles more likely to display reserve than

the others? _____

9. Which style is the opposite of the **S / Steadiness** style?

_____. Name two ways they are opposites.

_____, _____.

10. Which style is the opposite of the **C / Conscientious**

style? _____. Name two ways they are opposites.

_____, _____.

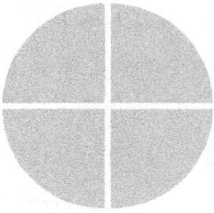

Chapter 9

The Blended DISC

IN 1928, the book *Emotions of Normal People* by William Moulton Marston ignited psychologists' interest in our subject, and research, studies and tests tried to build assessments to assist in analyzing human emotions. Early researchers came up with 15 patterns, then up to 60 patterns. What concerns us of course in this book are the *four* patterns that we have called **DISC**. The **DISC** approach has proven itself over time as a true measure and demonstration of all humans' behaviors.

From the 4 main patterns, we derive others through combining. You have surely already noted what your own blend is, as you took the Simple **DISC** or other online **DISC** assessments and read your results. Your results might show one, two or three of the styles as equally strong, while the remaining styles are (as they say in Hollywood and Bollywood) in a supporting role.

When we group the patterns together in pairs—**DI, DS, DC, SI, SC, IC**—we create what we call, for our purposes of illustration, **Blended Styles.** You may recall from my description of myself in the Preface, that I myself am the blended style of **SI**, and by now begin to put together a picture of what that, or your own blend, means.

80% of people testing their **DISC** patterns will have two strong styles, with the 20% blending three styles. In this chapter, I am not going to reiterate, for the most part, the style descriptions. You can refer to the chapters describing each of the four styles. Rather, I will tell you stories from my consultancy (all names changed!) that illustrate some blended styles. From there, you can study your own blend and arrive at your own conclusions as far as your needs for improvement or growth are concerned.

Max's DI Blend

This story is about an individual who tested out on the **DISC** as a strong **DI** blend—his **D** style was *as strong as* his **I** pattern. Keep in mind as you read that the **D** and **I** are both *fast-paced* styles, but they are opposites in that the first is *task-oriented* and the second *people-oriented*.

Max was from a company of 120 or so employees. The company had a Talent Pool whose task was to identify high-potential leaders within the company and further train them for positions in management. Its leaders had decided to put four employees, including Max, in the Talent Pool this particular year. This is why the company consulted with me. The individuals were section heads at the time and would train to become managers. They each sat for a **DISC** assessment, and did an 'intake' interview with the coach (me) and the general manager. The GM was impressed with Max, who was a results-oriented person, a self-starter and a multitasker, with superior skill in verbal communication. He had skill in managing a cross-functional team, and was a savvy, strategic thinker.

When analyzing his **DISC** assessment, he was a strong **DI** style. He was an influencer of other people, a great motivating speaker and fired people up. He loved a challenge and kept asking management for more and more work. However, when questioning his 25+ subordinates in a more or less informal way, it was quite difficult to get them to say anything negative or bad about him—they seemed afraid of him. Yet he was clearly results-oriented and effective when away from people and emotions.

The assessment was that Max was a top management pleaser from his strong **I** and with his **D's** love of a challenge, ability to handle a big work load and achieve results. However, Max was very aggressive and impatient from his strong **D** with his subordinates. And that needed further work! A '360 Degree Feedback' was suggested, and finally agreed by the client for Max.

A '360 Degree Feedback' gives employees (in this case, Max) anonymous feedback from the people who work around them—up and down the hierarchy. Those 'doing a 360 on Max' were his own manager, his peers (the other section heads), and his subordinates (the people he supervised and managed). The 360, due to its anonymity, was seen as a way of getting his subordinates to honestly open up, speak their mind, and have no concern about repercussions.

The results were clear: Members of top management were still very pleased with Max's performance. From his peers, the results were rather neutral. But from his subordinates—those he supervised and managed—he got rough scores. They scored him poorly. He was harsh with employees. He was poor with relationships. He was poor with sitting and coaching his staff. He never listened, pleading no time. He was only respected because of his position in the hierarchy! His staff did say that he verbally fired up and motivated them quite successfully, but after a while that just wasn't enough, given his other behaviors. The staff quickly lost trust in Max because he seemed to say one thing and do the opposite— probably as a result of his drive to please top management, even as he did his best to fire up his staff to get the results he needed to please that top management. He was an impatient person, and his subordinates stated that they heard him say, "I don't have the time for that" more than once—meaning he didn't have time for *them*. Subordinates stated that they loved the company, and had their own great ideas and wanted to make a contribution of those ideas, but Max had no patience to hear them out.

Well, Max was astounded at the commentary that resulted from his 360-feedback report. He was a good guy, honestly, yet his natural pace regarding 'getting things done' was so high-speed from his combined **D** and **I** that he left his staff behind—in the dust, as it were.

To his credit, he graciously accepted the results and the offered coaching. The coaching primarily entailed bringing his awareness to the *need for more of a balance between his two styles*. The high **D** style suited top management perfectly, but not his staff. Things were 'lopsided' in that respect. He needed to give feedback, and not bark it out. He needed to be more receptive of feedback and ideas from subordinates as their leader.

While his strong **D** had him actively achieving the results top management needed, his strong **I** was not listening to his subordinates. For his staff in particular, he needed to dial back his impatience and his continuous commands to 'do-do-get it done,' in favor of more often paying calm attention and actively listening to his staff members. He learned how to do 'active listening' which was a new skill for him. He learned to bite back his impatience, and go into a quieter, calmer mode. He needed to balance his seriousness and his lightness aspects—and the latter was suffering, so he focused on 'letting the fun out' more often.

We established a 'secret' development plan for him. We set one Listening Day each week for Max, during which he focused on exercising a *moderate pace* (unusual for his style, as both the **D** and **I** are fast-paced patterns). He also focused on being silent with his subordinates—listening without speaking or interrupting, and without impatient body language. He only spoke if it were to ask a pointed question to elicit more information, clarification or new ideas from his staff. As Max was also quite explosive, the second part of his coaching had him keep a little notebook in his pocket, in which he would simply mark an **X** each time he either 1) felt impatience, anger, or an explosion surging up within him or 2) actually let loose with that explosion.

This coaching and the expectations put on Max by me, his coach, were not explained or revealed to his subordinates. Max was to do this on his own, and after six months, his staff would be 'interviewed' through a new (and equally anonymous) 360 Feedback questionnaire.

The outcome? His staff noted dramatic, welcomed changes in Max! Max had achieved better balance between his two styles, and apparently a better grasp of when it was appropriate to 'release' each one. He was still results-oriented, but he had awareness of how to achieve a balance. He was getting better at his people-orientation, having realized how advantageous a 'tool' it was as a leader needing to coax productivity from two dozen people each day.

After this, he admitted to me privately that he had been behaving with the same imbalanced actions in his home—and there had always been trouble at home because of it. He had acquired— through the **DISC**, 360 Feedback and our coaching exercises—an understanding of *why* things were rocky at home. This was a big, big revelation for him!

He thanked me . . . more for saving his marriage than saving his career. As he watched his own behaviors, got training in all the **DISC** styles and came to identify his staffs' styles too, he understood better what was going on in <u>all</u> his relationships.

At work and at home, he has become more patient, a better listener, better able to slow down at will, and although it's always going to be a challenge for him, he tries to relax and open up to others' needs and motivations. Is he still results-focused? Yes! But he has more and better tools to achieve those results.

Max was open and willing to learn, become a better man, a better leader. His coaching created awareness, new tools and a sort of watchfulness. He knows that if things are rocky in any relationship at all, he pulls out his **DISC** knowledge, and is armed to shift things. Max is a terrific example of how willingness and awareness can change an entire life—not just one aspect or one relationship, but many.

Jasmine's SI Blend

I was conducting a training session during which each attendee did a **DISC** assessment. One of the quiet ladies in attendance, let's call her Jasmine, tested at an **SI** style, with each style being equally strong. Please recall that the **S** style is for *sweetness* and *support*, and is a *moderately-paced individual*. A strong **S** is 'beyond' people-oriented and moves into *relationship-orientation*, with *a few close relationships* being the heart of the **S's** life and attention. The **I** style is likewise people-oriented, but very *fast-paced*, in contrast to the **S**.

People liked her! She talked softly. She was magnetic, very supportive of everyone. People believed that whoever had married her must be in heaven! At the end of the course, she pulled me aside and begged me to create a second course to which she could invite her husband, let's call him Issac. She wanted me to come up with some argument that would convince Issac unequivocally to attend! I was surprised and asked her why she did not convince him herself, since she had such a soft, persuasive and magnetic way of speaking to others. I understood she did not like confrontation (just as a matter of knowing her **DISC** style . . . and being an **SI** myself . . .), and said to her, "Even if there is some discussion, surely you can bring him around and persuade him to register." "No," she insisted, "I need your assistance in getting him to attend." I knew this insistence was also typical of her **SI** style, which doesn't go directly to a solution but tries to find a workaround that won't hurt anyone's sensibilities.

I ultimately agreed to assist Jasmine and proposed attendance to her husband of 14 years at a 50% tuition rate for the very next training session, conditional on Jasmine also attending with him (which thrilled her). Issac accepted, and they both came. He tested as a strong **ID** individual. From his **D** aspect, he was verbally very direct, displaying high temper. Generally, he was very active, liked people and taking action. In their home life, Issac loved to gather lots of friends and family together on a regular monthly basis for events like picnics, and for all the years of their marriage, Jasmine had typically begged him to be more private, and to spend more quality time together with her and their children instead of these big group events . . . but then always bowed to his wishes. He loved those gatherings with friends and family and was blind, we must say, to the message Jasmine was trying in vain to send him!

He was initially surprised and disappointed to discover that his wife was a strong **SI**, until I reminded him that there are no good or bad behavior styles—only styles that need to be understood. What he understood, at long last, was that when he was pressing his wife to organize and attend these monthly big group, public gatherings with him that she was both supporting him . . . and suffering from that support! Her natural strong **S** tendency was to support his decisions, avoid conflict and confrontation with him, and keep the relationship with him strong. However, to create that, she went against her very behavioral nature. Ah! Issac's eyes opened.

Issac said to me, "My demanding, my ignorance—I never thought about her, honestly. Now I notice that she was avoiding conflict and confrontation about it. I see she was suffering. I need to sit with her." He left for a while to do that.

Later, I heard about their holiday. In all years past, he was the one deciding to gather friends and family to celebrate this particular holiday, with the pressure on Jasmine to make it a festive event. Now, with his new understanding of his spouse, he invited no one. He made it clear to Jasmine and his kids that this was a private, family-only event that for once they would celebrate together and on their own. Issac reported that he had an absolutely magical time with his family! Indeed, they were a close-knit, loving family, not in small part due to his wife's strong **S** traits and particularly her relationship-building tendencies (and now, as he understood, her strong relationship *preservation* tendency!).

Issac learned to balance his strong **I** and his imposing strong **D** with her strong **S**. He understood that for the entire span of their marriage, it had been Jasmine who had been adapting, and decided it was his turn now. He apologized to his wife and reiterated his love. He no longer created those large spontaneous events—now planned upon agreement with her—unless he gave her lots of time to prepare in all ways. He finally 'got' that his spouse was a strong finisher, but needed lots of time to get event planning or other change in her routine underway.

Jasmine feels that she reached her goal of expanding and deepening her already loving and trusting relationship with him. She feels her children have also benefited 'by osmosis' from their father's new understanding and personal efforts to 'invest' more in family.

I'm Quitting!

Instead of the dual style blend in one individual, I'd like to present a case where the sharp contrasts in **DISC** style between boss and assistant might jeopardize a whole career.

During a workshop I conducted, one of the attendees—let's call him Elias—had been planning to resign from his job as the executive assistant to one of his company's top executives.

He found himself unhappily stuck in his job position with a boss he couldn't figure out how to please. Elias experienced too much pressure at work trying to make the boss happy, and felt there were too many clashes with his boss. Elias didn't know how to deal with it.

At my workshop, he finally discovered himself ... and his boss (who was not even in attendance). Elias (not a **D** at all himself) realized he had a strong **D** boss with, as you now know, little-to-no people-orientation. Alongside his own **DISC** assessment, it explained everything to him, and suddenly Elias had some hope for his work life. At the workshop, we naturally not only tested and analyzed each one's own assessment, but got to understand each of the four styles, which is when he discovered his boss's style . . . in so many clear descriptive **D** words and Ah-Ha moments.

Elias was of a **DISC** style (I will let you determine which one) who would arrive at work, cheerfully greet and shake everyone's hands before getting down to work and preparing for his first meeting with his boss.

Elias understood that he was naturally a moderately-paced person who liked people. He also realized from our work at the seminar that his boss was a fast-paced **D**. The boss was task-oriented in contrast to Elias's own people-orientation. Ah— contrasts! The boss being faster-paced than Elias explained his impatience and the pressure he put on Elias to hurry up with tasks and projects. His boss was direct, (somewhat) dictatorial, and didn't like 'chit-chat.' He was a 'get-to-the-point' sort of man.

Armed with some suggestions from me and other attendees, and his new understanding of both of their behavioral patterns, Elias changed his approach at work—starting right after the seminar. Now, when going into meetings, Elias shifted his own behaviors to match his boss's a bit more. Instead of starting any meeting with his strong **D** boss with his usual handshaking and relationship-building conversation with the attendees, Elias just greeted everyone with a quick Hello, sat down, kept quiet and waited for the high **D** boss to get things going. He made sure that he assisted his boss through direct and very brief responses any time they were needed, rather than his usual long, drawn-out answers.

Elias also changed other habits at work. He no longer shook hands and greeted everyone and chatted right away upon arriving every morning, but went straight to his office, grabbed his agenda for the day and went to his strong **D** boss to review and discuss it in a brief, direct exchange. He would formulate brief and direct questions to ask his boss's goals, objectives and activities for the next meeting and the day. Only after that was done, would Elias return to his office, find his work friends, and greet and chat with them—just as if it was the beginning of their workday.

Of course, Elias noticed that his workmates were confused by this change. But they finally understood he was adapting to their boss's style; they observed the new comfort and even happiness that Elias exhibited on the job. Indeed, his boss so appreciated Elias's well-thought-out shifts in behavior that he recommended Elias as his own successor! Far from quitting his job, he was lined up for a promotion.

Elias was able to achieve this multifaceted result through an understanding of not only his own **DISC** behavior style, but his boss's. He was much more comfortable in all facets of his work due to this understanding. He was much more comfortable—and effective, in his boss's view—in all interactions with his strong **D** boss due to understanding 'where his boss was coming from' and how he was positioned in relation to his own style. Elias became a much more appreciated and effective assistant to this strong **D** boss, and he knows this because his boss stated as much!

By the way, since you have by now deduced that Elias came from a strong **S** style, how do you think he will do as his boss's successor? What do you believe his second strong style is that is paired up with that **S**?

More Awareness

In addition to those few stories from my case files, let me briefly give you some other examples of how the style blendings manifest in different individuals. My hope is that these illustrations will expand your awareness of human behavior, and your ability to detect combinations of the **DISC** behavior styles in others. My additional hope—and it is what I try to help people do every day—is that you willingly shift your behaviors, even momentarily, to get along with others of different styles from your own.

The SC Blend

In James, his strong **S** aspect means that he avoids/dislikes sudden change and any type of conflict; proposing a sudden change in his schedule to James is likely to put him in a cold sweat, not only because of his **S**, but also due to his **C** traits. Contrary to a pure strong **C**, he is chatty and loves to talk—that's because of his **S**. His **C** indicates his real technical expertise in his field, where he has been the go-to man for 30 years. His **C** also means that you can set your watch by what he does and when he does it—because his days are so regimented (again, no sudden changes in schedule for him!).

The DC Blend

We perceive a **D-C blend** in Janet. Her rather unilateral decision-making tendencies tune you in to the **D** side of her. She wants what she wants when she wants it! From her **C,** she expresses her need to preplan every task, trip or project—needless to say, her more "let's see how things go" spouse and Janet don't agree when it comes time for a vacation. For instance, he is willing to just see what lodging is available when they get to their nightly destination on a road trip, but Janet is compelled to call and book ahead . . . after grilling the hotel clerk for a dozen details. Her **C** also pushes her to achieve perfection as often as the context allows. Her husband and Janet studied their **DISC** together, and now they have ways that they bend and shift that work for them— they both feel more understood and heard by the other when they come from their natural styles.

The IC Blend

This is our friend Robert—a focused, out-of-the-box-thinking inventor. Robert's **I** is all about innovative, unconventional think-ing. His **I** style is the 'place' he gets all his ideas, concepts and vision for his inventions—and also allows him to be comfortable chatting enthusiastically with others about his invention and networking with the right people who just might buy it. He is so focused when in his **C** aspect, as he fiddles and experiments and builds his invention, that a stampede of wild horses could not distract him from the task at hand. His **C** gives him an ability to focus deeply; the **C** allows him to map out the details and steps necessary to create the invention.

The IS Blend

In the Preface, where I introduced myself, you may recall me stating that I was an **I-S**. Do you now know more about the **IS** blend (and how it is distinct from the **IC** blend discussed above)? You also, then, know more about me—before even meeting me. That is the beauty of the **DISC** behavioral styling!

Four Shared Searches

Chapters ago, I spoke about mankind's shared four searches. I noted philosophers' observations over millennia that we all seek 1) approval and acceptance, 2) personal control, 3) safety and security of our body and our possessions, and 4) a sense of oneness with the greater family of man.

You might have wondered as you read that how that perspective could fit into the **DISC** viewpoint of human behavior patterns. Here is a sampling of how that is so:

Remember the **Steadiness S** profile? Very people-oriented with strong tendency to build long-term relationships. Very emotional as well and very in tune with other people's feelings and desires. The **Influential I** is quite concerned that other people like them. All that sounds to me like 'seeking approval and acceptance' from others. Remember the **C Conscientiousness** profile? These individuals take criticism of their work product very badly, because they are so attached to getting it right and producing very accurate product for you. Taking criticism badly is an emotional aspect of 'seeking approval and acceptance,' don't you think?

The **C** wants to plan, plan, plan before starting any project, and the **Dominant D** needs to be in charge of all tasks she is ever involved in—doesn't that sound very much like 'seeking to control'?

The **C** dislikes sudden change as much as the **S** does, and that sounds a lot like 'seeking security and safety' in the status quo.

You can think of other ways each style seeks one of these shared outcomes. What about the fourth search for 'oneness with the greater family of man'? We really all want to get along with the people in our lives. We all really prefer harmony over discord, and love over hate, and cooperation over disunity and separation. This fourth search is for more unity. The challenge is that far too many people just don't realize how united we already really are, because what they perceive and focus upon are the *differences* rather than these *similarities*.

A Quiz
on Your Observations

LIST AT least four people who are closest to you. They can be family, friends, coworkers, business partners—as you like. Write their first names down in a list like mine below. As an example, I will use the four individuals who helped me present each of the four styles, plus a fifth person.

1. Jim	fast-paced	D/Dominant	D/I
2. Lizbet	fast-paced	I/Influential	I/S
3. Edoardo	moderately paced	S/Steady	S/C
4. Andrei	slow-paced	C/Conscientious	C/D
5. Guido	fast-paced	D/Dominant	D/?

A. After each name, write whether this person is **fast**-paced or (moderate) **slow**-paced.

B. Think about each one's **single** or **strongest behavioral style** right now. If you could only choose one behavior style for each person, which one would it be? Write it now, as I have on my list.

C. If you have two or more people on your list of the same predominant **DISC** style, like I do, can you name two ways that they are _different_ from each other? (I list two **D's**, and discuss their differences below).

D. Lastly, indicate what you think their dominant pair of styles might be—just from your observations.

For example, Jim is a strong **D**, and another individual I have listed in 5ᵗʰ place on my list, my good friend Guido (no, not his real name), is also a strong **D**. I have easily observed that Jim is notably **decisive** and a **driver**, while Guido is neither. However, Guido is most notably **dictatorial** and **domineering**—two traits not shared with Jim. While they are both strong **D** individuals, notice that Jim has a strong **I** (which probably has something to do with him not being very dictatorial or domineering . . .), but I am not sure that Guido has another style that is as strong or discernible (to my eyes) as his **D**.

Go ahead now and see if you can do something similar with your list.

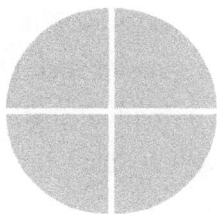

Chapter 10

Using the DISC to Improve Relationships

WHEN WE feel stuck by things happening a relationship, we ask ourselves how we can improve it—or how we can get out of the relationship entirely! It is fight-or-flight, isn't it? Fight for the relationship or flee it. . . .

How We Are Stuck

We can feel stuck in our relationships for a number of reasons. Perhaps at work we are stuck with a certain boss that we rarely agree with, or that we don't understand very well, or we just don't like. If we want to keep this job, we are stuck with that boss, and stuck in misunderstandings and uncomfortable interactions. We are trapped by the assignments we receive at work too, since it is almost impossible to refuse them, and we will like some of them and dislike others. We get stuck working with an individual that we just don't like. As leaders, we might get stuck with people who don't want to follow.

Even in a relationship we have chosen, such as a personal friendship, business partnership or marriage relationship, we feel unhappily caught up in repeated disagreements, in recurring high drama and emotions that we seem not to control, or in the need to deal with the fallout of occasional miscommunications and misunderstandings, and so on. Relationships are difficult!

Just on a personal level, we are also stuck with ourselves, as we tend to do things the same way over and over again, day after day—whether this is satisfactory to us or not. We are creatures of habit. Our habits become natural and comfortable to us quite quickly—but might seem confusing, aggressive, narrow-minded, exasperating (to name a few reactions) to other people.

From Stuck to Smooth Sailing

In chapter 1, I told you about six troubled or rocky relationships. These individuals felt trapped in communication styles and behaviors that were not working for any of them. I'd like to revisit them now, in light of your new knowledge about **DISC**, and help you see how effectively that new information about human behavior patterns can be used to improve those relationships.

Keep in mind, though, that every relationship between any two individuals you could name will be different from anything I present to you below. Add a third individual to the mix, and things become different yet again. Simply use these scenarios, in which I place the four behavioral styles and the task versus people orientation and fast versus slow tendency, to inspire you to make shifts and changes to improve your important relationships. Once you have fully discovered your own profile and the **DISC** profile of all the people important to you in your life, it will be easier than you think.

Also remember that our natural behavior style allows us to feel that we have *personal control* over our world, and thus we feel *comfortable* interacting in it. In rocky relationships, that control and that comfort have flown out the window . . . at least in our personal opinion! As you improve relationships through an understanding of each other's behavioral styles, and gentle adaptation to them when needed, what you are really doing is bringing back a sense of personal control and comfort *to each other*.

The first key, then, to improving relationships is first to know your own behavioral style, and of course to have knowledge of the other person's. The second key is a willingness to temporarily modify, shift or adapt your own natural or usual style to give the other individual that sense of control and comfort. In other words, you can shift even though the other person does not—and things will still improve!

Parent/Child Relationship

. . . .

YOU ARE a social, gregarious parent with a shy, quiet child. How do you connect with that child, and enjoy more open, two-way interactions with her? How can you understand each other, appreciate each other better?

. . . .

You the parent are probably a much stronger **I** or **S** style person than your child! You are very, very people- and relationship-oriented. The **I** style is gregarious, chatty, loves people and flits from one conversation and topic to another on a whim. The **S** in you is the part that says, "Oh, I don't want to hurt my child's feelings! Feelings are important." Both the **I** and the **S** are people-oriented and outgoing.

What about your child, then? 'Shy and quiet' sound like a **C** individual to me. A **C** is reserved (contrasted to you who are outgoing). A **C** is not people-focused like you are, but task-oriented. A **C** is not so much shy (as **I or S** people will see him) as he is reserved and quiet by nature. That is a strong **C** style.

Let's say your child is too young right now to understand the **DISC** approach. You, however, are not! It is thus your responsibility to shift your own naturally outgoing and chatty behaviors when interacting with this quiet child of yours. Push your **S** to listen even more than you typically would. Listen actively. Repeat what he's said, and ask how he feels about that. Then be *physically and verbally quiet and listen* some more. Don't let the **I** part of you interrupt your child, or act impatient as you wait for him to formulate his answers, and definitely refrain from answering for him (which is just the same as interrupting). You will need to give this child lots of time to talk with you, lots of time to get going on and complete tasks. Don't suddenly shorten a pre-announced deadline from your own **I** impatience—you'll end up sending your **C** child into a corner and he'll be ruffled that you didn't let him do it his way. His way is slow—much, much slower than either your **I** or **S** styles do things. Give him time. Give him silence (and no hopping around while you are waiting and no surfing on your smartphone, either—he needs 100% of your direct attention) to prepare and state his ideas. Things will go better between you.

Sibling Relationship

YOUR YOUNGER sister is a wild child, willing to try everything once and to break the rules to do so. You have tried to change her, and that obviously is not working. How do you, her rule-following, parent-obeying older brother worried about her getting into trouble (or worse) not only share your concerns with her so that she listens, but get her to behave more 'like you'? Or can you?

Let's face reality. The same mother and father with a number of children will be quite likely to discover that each one of those children has a different **DISC** style. Yes, the children share many qualities and experiences with each other and their parents (similar physical traits or body language, shared values and beliefs, etc.), yet have their own unique blend of behavioral styles that sets them apart from their siblings. It is this very unique blend that each possesses that leads them to get along or throws them into disagreement with each other.

In this scenario, the younger sister is probably a strong **I** and a strong **D**. Neither of these styles like to follow rules! The strong **I** part of the younger sister is willing to try everything once from sheer curiosity, creativity and daring. The strong **D** part of this little sister is what leads her to say, "Don't tell me what to do!" or "I know what I'm doing, leave me alone."

I suspect the obedient older brother might be a blend of a strong **C** and a slightly weaker **S**. The **S** part of her brother is what leads him to 'help her get back on the right path' because he'd be devastated for her if she got into any real trouble. It is the stronger **C** part of him that dictates what that 'right path' is! His strong **C** knows what the rules are and finds great comfort in respecting them. He just can't understand why little sister is so happy to break the rules.

Since the brother is the older sibling here, let's have it be the brother who makes shifts and adaptations in his own style to get along better with his younger sister. What should he do? First, he needs to recognize her need to be fast-paced and doing lots of things seemingly at one time (contrary to his own style) and also to do things her way with little oversight or accountability to him (her strong **D**).

He needs to step back and allow his sister to learn from her potential mistakes and use her strong **D** to take charge a little better. He needs to tell her that he trusts her to do the right thing—because that speaks to her strong **D**! Since little sister's strong **I** is people-oriented, brother can encourage little sister to let him or their mother know when she will be back home, or who she thinks she will spend time with that day. In any case, we are creating a scenario in which the brother feels a little calmer about his sister's apparent recklessness. With her strong **D** (task-oriented) understanding his request, hopefully little sister will humor her brother by doing as he asks . . . at least once.

In conversation, he could ask her to tell him about that creative new thing she has been discovering lately—that will comfort his strong **S** for relationship-building and comfort her strong **I** because she gets to talk excitedly about her happy and creative experiences.

Now keep in mind that the opposite scenario exists, too. That is, it is big brother who is the rule-avoiding **I** and the younger sister is the rule-abiding **S**. Do you automatically think that this is 'better' because a male can take care of himself better than a female? Don't! Culturally, we might tend to jump to such types of conclusions, but have no judgements about good or bad, better or worse. This is just how it is!

When the Boss Does Not Lead

. . . .

THE BOSS is supposed to be a leader, right? Unfortunately, in our workplaces that is not always the case. Many of us are trapped with supervisors or managers who don't naturally know how to get along, and with whom we have no effective communication. What can you do, as that boss's supervised employee, to help the team's members do your jobs right . . . without going over his head or making him look bad?

. . . .

I often see some version of this communication 'disconnect' in our workplaces. We usually expect the boss to step up and make behavioral shifts that facilitate two-way communication and erase miscommunication. It is not always possible. So you step up instead.

First look informally—using your new knowledge—at the boss's probable **DISC** profile. From what you have learned in the prior chapters of this book, you can probably identify at least one strong behavioral style for this individual. You can also certainly identify his task-versus-people focus as well as his fast-versus-slow pace preference.

My guess is that he is not a people-oriented individual even though that would obviously be beneficial in his leadership role. But don't condemn him yet! Perhaps the work you and your team do under his supervision is quite *task-oriented*, and his own bosses think he's the best guy they have!

This said, what do you now know about the boss and his **DISC** style, pace and focus?

If your boss is not people-oriented like you, how can you smooth things over between him and other team members without disrespecting him? My advice is to do it in front of the boss. When the boss has given his brief instructions and everyone on the team is looking confused, just step up and ask your boss, "If I understand correctly, sir, you mean ___. Is that correct or not?" If your boss is task-oriented, he will appreciate your very specific question. It will give him an opportunity to respond with a specific new explanation. Whether he is a stronger **D** or a stronger **C** (our two task-oriented styles), this approach will work.

Then you ask him your next very concise question, and your next—with your last question directed to your fellow team members: "Have I forgotten anything, guys?" Hopefully, other team members will have jumped in with a question or two of their own. In any case, don't be too heavy-handed with this. You don't want your boss thinking that you are taking over his job! Just be gently helpful for your confused coworkers. Then move on, to perform the tasks at hand.

Know-It-All Authority Figures

· ·

PHYSICIANS ARE quite the authority figure around the world. Do we need to remain trapped in such one-way interactions, most especially when it has become clear that it is not to our benefit? Let's face it, sometimes the authority has missed something important! Your father is quite ready to believe what his doctor says without question or challenge. However, your dad is not getting better—in fact, from your observations, his condition is worsening even as he follows 'doctor's orders.'

· ·

You have always been skeptical of all authorities' statements and believe in doing your own research. When your father's health condition gets worse, how do you get the know-it-all, ego-centric doctor to hear what you have to say from your own research . . . in defense of your father's health and very life?

This is a real experience one of my associates had with his own father, and his father's physician. Here is what happened.

The adult son had to deal with the behavior styles and expectations and beliefs of two individuals: his father and the physician. The son figured that his father was a strong **C** blended with an **S** that was nearly as strong—the **C** in him was compliant with authority, rules and prescriptions made by people in authority; the **S** part of his style was willing for his son to help him, willing to engage in substantive new conversation with the physician . . . but he was indecisive about doing so.

The son figured the doctor for a strong **D** combined with a strong **C**. A professional who was not good with people and not much of a give-and-take conversationalist (the reserved aspect of the **D** and **C**), but great at the specific tasks involved with becoming and being a doctor (his task-orientation aspect).

My friend thought he had discovered a heart issue in his dad's symptoms. The physician had not been looking for heart or circulatory system problems at all. The son knew he had to make his case clearly, point by point, and had to do it in few words. The doctor would rebel against a non-doctor diagnosis, so he had to appeal to the physician's strong **C**—use of logic, process and procedure (the medical and lab testing that was available) to confirm or infirm his opinion. The doctor was both reluctant and flattered in the end, most fortunately! Reluctant (from his 'don't tell me what to do' **D** aspect) and flattered (from his strong **C's** conscientiousness and compliance side). He ordered the tests requested by the son. They came back affirming the son's suspicions of heart disease and obstruction. The doctor immediately sent the father into surgery (in fact, the same day) which saved the man's life.

This is a true story! Save a life. Learn **DISC**. Learn how to be the 'behavioral interpreter.'

I'm Filing for Divorce!

• •

BOTH YOU and your spouse have been thinking that you are on the verge of divorce. You seem to communicate at cross purposes. You seem to have contrary expectations of each other's role in the relationship. Nothing one says is well-received (or understood, in many cases on both sides) by the other. What a painful situation when you feel trapped in a relationship that has gone from sweet to sour! But . . . men are from Mars and women are from Venus—so there is nothing else to be done, right?

• •

Wrong! Don't file for divorce yet. Or . . . ever. Indubitably, learning about **DISC** styles and both sharing and applying the information in this book is a far better solution.

The challenge? It can be as simple as one spouse being a strong **C** and the other being a strong **I**—and neither of them knowing this! From your current knowledge of human behavior styles, you know that the **C** and the **I** are 'opposites' of each other as far as behavior styles go. Remembering this explains many things right away! From your knowledge of **DISC**, you see how these two individuals appear to be quite opposite.

The **C** is quite a reserved and shy individual who doesn't easily engage in conversation or in groups of people; a **C** has limited body movement and tight body language. The **I**, quite the contrary, is outgoing and talkative, a real whirlwind of physical movement and expressiveness.

The **C** is strongly task-oriented, and is the consummate rule-follower. The **I** comes from a very strong people-orientation, and hates rules.

The **C** is most comfortable with tried-and-true processes and procedures, with following step-by-step instructions. The **I** puts more importance on personal creativity and satisfying curiosity than on instructions or processes to be followed or rules to be obeyed.

How could this play out in a marriage relationship, when 1) both know about **DISC** versus when 2) neither one knows anything about behavior patterns and adaption techniques? Do you see how different things could be?

If the **I** spouse is the husband . . . the **C** wife complains that she cannot get him to do things like repairs around the house, or shopping for a specific list of items after work. At least not on her timetable or without her constant reminders. The **C** wife cannot get her husband to arrive places on time or pay the bills when they are due. He has so little regard for time, and for how things should be!

From the **I** husband's perspective, he and his wife won't be able to go out for a lively evening of 'fun' with friends—she never seems to enjoy it nearly as much as he does. Quite the contrary, she sits in her chair, quietly waiting for it to be time to go home. She always complains about his unkempt appearance and wild combinations of unpressed clothes. She is too demanding on him to get things done around the house . . . but what is the hurry?

In some cases, luckily, I have seen that complete awareness of each other's **DISC** behavior styles is enough to wake a married couple up. It is like a light bulb going off over each of their heads! Love and new respect come rushing back into the relationship! They see with some relief that their marriage, their relationship, is not really broken. Nonetheless, they each need to make gentle shifts in their usual behavior styles in order to get along over time. They each need to be not only willing but able to change old habits and patterns.

In our story here, what could those gentle shifts be comprised of?

Perhaps one discussion they could have is whether they need to *reverse traditional marital roles*. Why would this shock? In the comfort of your own home, you want to create comfort—and that is just what occurs when each individual is allowed to express himself or herself via the natural behavioral style. Traditionally, in other words, the man of the house performs or oversees the repairs. The man of the house traditionally makes sure the bills are paid. (These are of course my assumptions for the purpose of this scenario).

Perhaps this husband, with his strong **I**, needs to pass these responsibilities to his strong **C** spouse! If she is unable to do a repair herself, for instance, they will discuss a *process* for her to follow (because she is task- and process-oriented) that allows her to select and manage a contractor doing such repair work on their behalf. Will she need to get approval of the expense from her husband (part of her *process* that he talks about and agrees to with her)? If the husband decides that as the main money-earner of the family, he does need to become responsible for bill paying and general money-management, they might jointly decide that she sets the schedule (again, task-oriented for her; and he is off the hook for watching the calendar) for these payments, puts out all the paperwork for him, and sits and chats with him as he does it. What an opportunity for a quiet conversation, which the strong **I** husband loves, and which gives the routine-focused **C** a specific event to look forward to with him!

These are just a few ways that knowing each other's behavioral style can help both of you get creative in how you organize your shared life and get along terrifically well together! It is about creating a <u>comfort</u> zone and a sense of personal <u>control</u> *for each of you.* Just as people are different behavioral blends, so are marriages. Talk. Write things down. Respect each other's style, but also be 100% willing to bend and shift it when needed.

Parental Authority

I presented a parent/child *communication* issue as our first story of this chapter. But *authority* (or *boundaries)* is perhaps an issue in the family at times as well.

• •

AS THE head of your household, you are quite willing and able to take charge and make the decisions for everyone. You are totally flustered by your daughter's tearful protest that you are not taking everyone else's opinions into account. What is a father to do when his child feels trapped in unwanted situations like this—and you are stuck in your own habits and expectations?

• •

The father can learn about **DISC**! And so should his spouse and all of his children.

When a child rejects your authority in actions or just quietly questions it with words, there can naturally be a number of reasons. Children are no fools! If you arbitrarily impose certain rules with no reasonable foundation or justification for them, expect a revolt. However, in my experience, there are just as many instances of miscommunication through misunderstanding of each other's behavioral styles, motivations and needs.

If you have been paying attention until now, you probably realize that this man's daughter is a strong **S**. A strong **S** can quickly push into her extreme of being very emotional, tearful and defensive of others whom she loves. This family has a strong **D** father.

The **S** and the **D** are opposite behavioral styles, so doesn't that help right away to explain some of this friction? It should! The father's **D** is this **S** child's opposite behavioral style, and thus we arrive at a need for much awareness of and care with each other's style, motivators and needs—and a willingness to gently adapt *from both sides* in order to get along.

The **S** daughter needs to be made aware particularly of the differences between her father's **DISC** style and her own. Teach her that he is not a **D** 'because he is the father'—he is a **D** simply . . .

because! She needs to be reminded (or taught) that 'different' is not good or bad—it is just life! Perhaps as a minor child, she also needs to understand that although her father henceforth agrees to hear out everyone's opinions on any issue up for a decision in the family, she must expect that he will make the final decision on his own in the family's best interests. She must understand that that is her father's role as he perceives it and has created it within his family unit.

On the father's side of things, he needs to recognize that he is a task-focused individual while his daughter is very focused on people and relationships—and by extension on feelings that people are experiencing. Even though feelings are not much of a concern for this father as a strong **D** style, he hopefully becomes a little more willing and a little more able to take his family members' feelings into account on issues of importance. He should learn to say things like, "I hear your opinions about this; I see that you have strong feelings about this; let me think it over; please trust me to make a decision in our collective best interest."

DISC is about facilitating communication between people with very different behavioral styles, needs, motivations, fears and expectations. It seems apparent that a strong **D** like this father is behaviorally better equipped to make decisions than to his hedging, people-pleasing strong **S** daughter, but . . . not always! Beware of such assumptions.

Keep in mind the possibility of family units where the styles are reversed—a strong **S** head of household, with strong **D** children! That's a whole different scenario that I'll let you figure out for yourself, naturally based on your new knowledge of **DISC**!

DISC Mastery

Emotional Intelligence, or EQ, might be something you have heard about. It is not 'brain smarts' but 'relationship smarts,' and mastering the **DISC** will easily help you develop a higher EQ—if you use your **DISC** knowledge to observe other people and to improve your interactions with everyone.

The key to mastering any skill or making it a new habit is *repetition*. Just use the skill! Make mastering **DISC** a game. As you watch public leaders or celebrities in the media, try to determine which of the four **DISC** styles their responses, actions and reactions originated in. If you work and attend team meetings, or sit regularly with family at meals, do the same—every time someone speaks, intervenes, uses a particular type of body language or verbal language, comes or goes . . . use all this information to determine which of the four **DISC** styles they are behaving from. What is their blend of **DISC** styles? If you have judgements about their behavior, ask yourself why. Is it because their style is the opposite of yours? Or that they are not acting as *you* expect them to (that is, like you would)? Just notice. And practice adapting to their style for better outcomes.

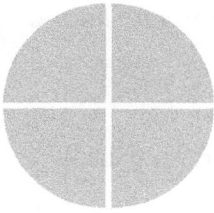

Chapter 11

Using the DISC to Change Your Own Behaviors

"What is necessary to change a person is to change his awareness of himself."

ABRAHAM MASLOW

YOUR SINGLE-MOST important life skill is your ability to create, manage and interact through relationships with people who are quite likely to be different from you in some major or minor way. 'Successful communication' is required to get what you need and want from the world and the people in it—not just once, but day after day. It is also indubitably needed when you want harmonious relationships.

Don't you find it amazing that wherever we live on the planet no one teaches this all-important skill set of 'relationship and communication' to us in school or in the home in any kind of formalized manner?

That means that we are virtually on our own not only to *figure out* but to *develop* 'good interpersonal communication' capability. That includes verbal and body language appropriate to the person we want to connect with, and appropriate to the circumstances. We are likewise on our own to *understand* what makes 'a good relationship' (not only in our terms, but as perceived by others) and how to create and maintain only that type of relationship. Luckily, we have the **DISC** methodology at our fingertips. How fortunate that it is not only so exact, but so readily available to all of us!

Permanent Change

I have given you some hints and clues in the previous chapter as to how people might shift out of their own usual behavioral styles into 'adaptive' behaviors in order to interact more smoothly and happily with others. Now it is time for me to answer a different question that I am frequently asked:

> *How can I use my own **DISC** results to help me **change** some of my behaviors which are not so positive?*

This question invariably arises once people have understood that they cannot *make* other people behave or act differently; we just cannot make others behave according to our own preferences and expectations. The question also arises once people understand that they are directly responsible for *their own* behaviors, responses and reactions in any circumstance—and that it is their own pattern that they control and can change to great benefit.

When you understand **DISC** and use it to improve your relationships, you are not changing yourself in a permanent way. I hope I have made that clear. You are temporarily modifying, adapting or shifting your usual behavior patterns to help the other individual feel more comfortable and in control, to enjoy a smoother communication or interaction—for all the benefits that brings to all parties involved. Those shifts you make are contextual. That means they will depend on the circumstances *at the time*.

This said, the question in this chapter is really about *permanent* change of one or more of your own tendencies. It is about personal growth, personal improvement through a decision for change. It is the question asked by people who really do want to make a real change in some specific (and uncomfortable or embarrassing) aspect of their usual behavior style. If you have detected an unwanted tendency, you can eliminate it. Up to you.

Awareness First

The first step in making any permanent change is awareness. If you are not aware that one of your usual behaviors repeatedly sabotages your credibility, your interactions or entire relationships, you cannot do anything about it. All too often, someone close to us (or perhaps a stranger who is simply a better observer than we are) will call our attention to a negative tendency of ours—and we get defensive. We go into denial. We revolt. We break down in tears. We turn on our heel and walk away to hide somewhere away from everyone.

What we need to do is just admit that there *might* be some truth in the observation. And if there is truth in it, do we really need to change it?

Willingness Next

Raw awareness is one thing, but if you are in denial that a trait of yours is somehow sabotaging you or holding you back in life, or reject that it is important to do something about it to preserve an important relationship—well, you won't make any change, will you? Likewise, a position that "It's their problem to accept me the way I am" is not conducive to making a change within yourself. If you cannot (or won't) change yourself, you certainly cannot change anyone else. Stop being defensive! No one out there is asking you to change—*you are asking you to change!*

It has been my experience that once we have seen *how* we could benefit from this one change, and expressed willingness (rather than denial or defensiveness) to do so, the ways and means show up.

Interruptions

One of my clients was repeatedly called to task by her supervisor and peers for rudely *interrupting* during meetings. She just couldn't help herself. Sometimes she would interject things to be humorous and to get attention. Sometimes she would interrupt to share her own opinion on the subject at hand (generally contradictory to the one being expressed). And sometimes, she would just mutter out loud and distract whoever was speaking and everyone who was listening. Not only her supervisor but her peers were getting exasperated at this irritating inclination of hers.

For a very long while, she was solidly in denial about their accusation of being an interrupter—she refused to believe that she was doing this. Then one of her peers had the idea of secretly recording an entire meeting that she participated in and playing it back to her . . . in front of everyone who had participated in that meeting. Wow! That is when the light bulb went off over her head! She finally understood *what* everyone was accusing her of. She finally understood how embarrassing that trait really was.

She became aware of the issue—"Yes, I interrupt repeatedly and rudely." And only after that, did she become aware of a need for change—"Yes, my credibility and my friendships and my job are at risk here. I must change."

And by the way, which of the four behavior styles was she probably exhibiting as an interrupter? I leave it to you to review your new knowledge of our four **DISC** styles and name it!

Know Thyself

You now have an example of how awareness of your **DISC** profile can reveal to you some negative (or simply unwanted) habits or tendencies of yours. Think about your own **DISC** profile now. Did you cringe as you read some 'negative' or embarrassing trait that described you perfectly? Is it bad enough or embarrassing enough to move you to analyze it, fix it, master it or erase it, and in that way make a permanent change?

That will always be up to you. However, if you break down in emotional tears with very little provocation in any public setting . . . if your out of control anger far too often frightens your family members (or puts them in physical jeopardy) . . . if your number one response in face of all challenges or criticism is to silently retreat and close the door . . . if your reaction is to resist at every turn . . . are these problematic enough for you to want to make a permanent change? Lots of unpredictable things happen in life and a lot of events will be out of your control, sabotaging your efforts, turning your life upside-down. Why be *your own* saboteur?

No one else can ever make such changes for you, as I stated above. It is a personal choice, a personal journey. Such decisions must come from within you and your heart of hearts. Such decisions come, often, from asking hard introspective questions:

→ How many people am I hurting with my negative
   habit when I am finally honest about it?

→ Am I hurting my advancement in my career because of this one negative trait, whatever it may be?

→ Am I jeopardizing one very important relationship (or many)?

→ Is this undesirable trait putting at risk the harmony and safety of my own home and family?

→ What about my own happiness in my relationships?

→ What about my sense of place in the world?

Only you can answer such questions.

Simply become aware. From awareness, you can decide if you are willing to act. From willingness, you find a process or method—as did our friend, 'The Interrupter.'

"Awareness without action is worthless."
Dr. Philip McGraw

Back to the Interrupter

The client who became aware of her tendency to interrupt—who finally admitted the truth of it—came to a personal decision. She would totally erase that tendency from her 'repertory' of behaviors. It took her about a year. Her process was fairly simple. But it wasn't easy! Here is what she did:

1) She imitated her peer, and for three months audio-recorded every conversation, business and private, short or long, that she had with anyone.

2) She ruthlessly replayed every conversation in the evening (and never skipped an evening). As she listened, she noted not only the number of times she interrupted, but tried to decipher the *trigger* to her interruptions. What led her to jump in with words? Was there a pattern? She discovered that it was another negative trait of hers called *impatience* that led her to interrupt over 75% of the time. (Which behavioral style(s) was she deeply rooted in with her impatience and interruption tendencies?)

3) For the rest of the year, every single time she felt the urge to speak, she bit her tongue (literally) and simultaneously relaxed her entire body with a technique learned from a meditation teacher. She did this whether she was *invited* by someone else to speak or was *tempted* to spontaneously interrupt. Both moves were to remind her of her

impatience. Both taught her that the world would not end if she did not speak! Her goal was to develop a new habit of 'thinking before speaking.'

4) She additionally set a negative incentive for herself. Yes, punishment! Every time she slipped up and interrupted someone, she'd pull out a little notebook and write an X. Then, for every X in her booklet at the end of the week, she had to put €5 into her savings account. Needless to say, at the start of this negative incentive exercise, her savings account grew quite a lot! That didn't matter to her. Making progress was the key.

This task-oriented individual came up with a process, all on her own. It had additional benefits for her that included better relaxation, better sleep, more self-assurance (she didn't have to speak all the time to feel respected; indeed, her silence was a new communication tool for her!), heightened thinking power and mental sharpness, and improved professional credibility from all her business relationships. Her boss and peers applauded her decision to make improvements and quietly supported her efforts.

I understand that you might need help to find a process. First comes awareness. Second comes the willingness to change and the decision to do so. Only then can you come up with a process that you will stick with so that it works for you.

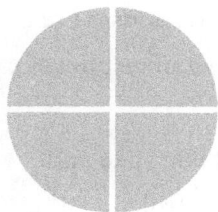

Chapter 12

A Review of Other Assessment Tools

DISC REVEALS your behavioral *temperament, style and tendencies.* I believe in its effectiveness to help people in so many ways, that I am often tempted to recommend only the **DISC**. **DISC** is a terrific tool to learn about yourself as an individual, to position yourself more beneficially in relation to others. It is also a great way to learn about and develop your leadership capabilities and needs, to provide support to you or your organization in job/team placement or career selection, to guide you in your personal and work interactions and behaviors—a tool for all purposes, really.

Remember that how we respond to situations is called our 'behavior.' **DISC** tells you how your own unique style *responds to situations or contexts.* **DISC** is about responses, how we respond, and gives us clues about our needs and some of the triggers that motivate or demotivate us. We have seen how our responses are a matter of the current context. We all have three types of responses:

1. Our '**usual**' behaviors—our most comfortable state and style, in which we feel we have the most control.

2. Our '**adaptive**' behaviors—those temporary shifts we consciously make to get along or better communicate with others of different styles.

3. Our '**extreme**' behaviors—those we deploy when we are pushed out of our comfort zone and/or feel we are losing or have lost control.

Which type will apply depends on the context or circumstances we are experiencing. Our perception of that context will be different from the view of a person of another behavioral style, as we have seen.

Other Assessment Tools We Have

Sometimes you or your organization have a specific purpose or need better addressed by a specialty assessment. There are many assessment tools on the market today. Some are specialized for the workplace only. Others are more generally applicable to a personal, family or community environment. I am only giving you a taste of some of these assessments in the section below. If your organization needs assistance in selecting the best one for your purposes or needs, you can get in touch with me and I can help.

Some assessments are appropriate for the work environment only and are used in gaging career placement, progress and performance. Other assessments are focused on leadership strengths and weaknesses, such as the **John Maxwell Leadership Assessment**, which uses five levels of leadership and measures 64 attributes in relation to success in leadership. If it is a performance assessment provided by your entire work team that you wish to measure, a **360-Degree Feedback** process might be the most appropriate tool.

Myers-Briggs Type Indicator

Called the **MBTI**, it is founded on the work of psychologist Carl G. Jung. It is famous in the work environment, but going out of favor in business in spite of decades of loyal usage. MBTI has been used as well in academia and in personal coaching. It strives to make Jung's 'psychological types' understandable by identifying and sorting out your preferences, without accounting for traits, abilities or character within you. It could give a psychological self-analysis to help you understand your reactions and responses to stressors or pressure (including in team or group situations).

Strong Interest Inventory (SII)

The **Strong Interest Inventory**, developed in the 1920s like other tools and revised most recently in 2004, is used almost exclusively in career assessment. If making a good career choice is your sole motivation for doing an assessment, it gives you insights into your interests so that you have less confusion in deciding on an appropriate career or profession for yourself.

StrengthsFinder 2.0

StrengthsFinder, or CliftonStrengths, is both an assessment *test* to determine what you naturally do best and a *guide* in developing the personal strengths you have discovered. It is user-friendly and is thus a good starting place for a general public reader. It is a print book, by authors Marcus Buckingham and Donald Clifton.

Why Groups Use These Tools

The above list is just a sampling of tests and tools that have been created to help us understand ourselves better and achieve personal and relationship improvement.

You have certainly deduced some of the reasons that your business, professional organization or family—or just you on your own—may ask a consultant to administer a personality, strengths or behavioral assessment. Although as you have read these pages many of those reasons seem to pop out as obvious, other reasons are quite subtle.

- **Relationship Counseling**, either in the family or in the workplace, and typically when a pair of individuals refuse to understand and adapt sufficiently for the relationship to be easy and harmonious.

I believe you have understood, not only from the entire book but especially from my numerous examples in Chapter 9, how doing a **DISC** profile for all your family members can assist you all in determining how to get along, communicate better, organize and deal with shared work and even jointly manage crises. There are versions of **DISC** for children, students and family relationships.

Couples often just need knowledge. **DISC** provides knowledge about self and other, as we have seen. Interpersonal awareness can be learned! Then couples practice how to adapt their natural styles, how to use each other's motivators more often and avoid the demotivators and so on, to create better communication, trust and respect.

Children will benefit from assessments written at their level of language knowledge. They gain understanding of their natural fears, needs and their own 'normal'. They grasp what their personal strengths are and how to manage their weak points. Of course, they learn how to approach and communicate with others, and deal with conflict as it arises.

Older children who are still students benefit from the self-awareness it provides. They can improve their grades through clarity about their preferred style of learning, along with the added motivational boost that self-knowledge provides. Young people learn how to work through interpersonal conflicts, and by learning about the **DISC** styles exhibited by others, nip many conflicts in the bud. Knowing their **DISC** style allows them to move into their strengths solidly and manage their weak points. Thus, it can help them set great achievable goals within the context of their natural style, such as preparing for a post-school career or other types of planning for their future.

Workplace Supervisors and Employers: Please Note!

Before I go on to explain other reasons to do assessments, I must interject this: **DISC** can also be performed on an *actual job position* (rather than only on the person, as we have been discussing up until now). When you have the **DISC** requirements of a job position, you can more easily do the person-to-job match-up. Efficiency skyrockets; productivity comes faster to new hires who are well-suited to the job at hand. You are also less likely to let a newly hired employee go and do some rehiring—a well-matched employee stays in the job much longer. He is simply like a happy fish in water (his natural context), rather than a fish that flopped out of the fish tank and cannot find its way back in (very uncomfortable, experiencing a loss of personal control).

A diverse team made up of **D, I, S,** and **C** individuals is very much the rule in workplaces—the trick is to help everyone appreciate and understand this diversity and work well together. **DISC** knows this and thus provides reports for supervisors with plenty of tips and techniques to use to get along with supervised individuals, help those employees perform more happily and effectively, get along with other team members and more.

Employers, Human Resource Managers, and Counselors can get in touch with me for details.

More Reasons to Do an Assessment

- **Recruitment Accuracy**, where a recruiting manager seeks to 'match' the personality as best as he can to the position. The theory is that happiness on the job, productivity and efficiency at work are a 'package deal' for which personality is the motor. Many companies won't hire anyone without such a test, and won't hire unless the results represent 'a good match.'

- **Employment Testing**, similar to above, but not yet for a specific job offer. The testing agency will try to determine the type of work, work environment and so on the candidate is best suited to from a personality perspective—all the while factoring in the individual's skills, talents and experience.

The premise of using assessments for the related activities of recruitment, employment? It is that someone displaying, for instance, a creative, innovative and people-oriented behavior *preference* might not be happiest or most productive working in a desk job doing computer tasks on his own all day. (Do you recognize the *I* not being happy in a perfectly *C* job?) Companies which systematically use these kinds of preliminary processes have systematically found that they make fewer hiring mistakes—and thus save lots of money in their recruiting process! They discover that they retain such 'well-matched' employees much longer than without an assessment. Less rehiring means less money spent by the company to correct past hiring mistakes.

- **Career Counseling**, either for those changing careers or for those not thriving in their current career and requiring assistance to uncover the reasons for this.

Just like any relationship, a career path can be sabotaged or propelled by an astute understanding of one's behavior style and a seriously honest assessment of one's 'pain points', so to speak (like our Interrupter friend). A career grows as the individual grows, and being aware as well as willing to make a few necessary adjustments or outright changes can move you faster and more happily along your chosen path.

- **Performance Assessment**, as achieved by a 360-Degree Feedback process.

After some time in a job position, your employer will want to gage how you are performing. With a 360-degree review, you are simply asking your peers, your supervisor(s), those you supervise, and those you otherwise work indirectly with to write a review based on a specific questionnaire. It is subjective, yes. But much can be learned by asking others how you are doing!

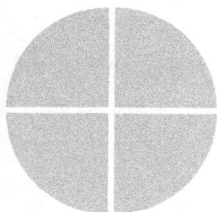

Chapter 13

Patterns and Improvements

"Know that people are doing the best they can from their level of awareness. Accept people for who they are and always be ready to forgive."

DEEPAK CHOPRA

USING THE DISC tool helps us internally and externally.

Internally, **DISC** allows you to get to know yourself much better. Understanding yourself is not as instinctive or automatic from birth as some skeptics of such assessments would like us to believe! Knowing yourself is also never a 'one-time-and-done' thing, but a lifelong process, as you observe yourself act and react in a wider and wider range of contexts.

Knowing which of our four behavioral styles describes you best—and how the four styles are blended within you—is a great start to having 'scientific' proof of your tendencies and motivations, understanding your needs, seeing all your strengths, your weak points, and even negative aspects. All these are dependent on context, of course, and you learn that as well.

I have witnessed a number of individuals who were so relieved (some to the point of breaking down in tears of relief) to finally understand how they are 'wired' in **DISC** terms. They finally recognized what moved them and others to do or say things when before, they were utterly perplexed and felt like some 'invisible hand' was driving this or that action or reaction. I even had a gentleman say to me that he now understood that there wasn't some '2nd person' hidden deep inside him doing crazy things. It was simply a second behavior style that popped up circumstantially!

Externally, **DISC** trains you in four revealing human *patterns* of behavior and their combinations, and allows you to better understand all the behaviors displayed by the people you work with (and who work for you) and all the people in your private life. Likewise, it is a good place to start for those wishing to improve or heal relationships, or develop new ones that are not only mutually beneficial, but thrive from the very start.

More Patterns

Entire organizations have been founded on the **DISC** premise of matching behavior styles to the mission of the group and its needs.

I know of an insurance company which was founded with an overseas investor. The lead man—the founding President—knew about behavior assessment tools from previous work and believed in them. He consulted to discover which **DISC** profiles to look for in each of the job types his company would be requiring. As it happened, his business, by its very nature, needed many quite strongly **C**-style professionals! His management team needed to be both people- and task-*understanding*. Notice I did not say 'oriented,' because a blend of those two factors was sought—and found in great people with the right management expertise. The president himself brought a trio of strengths in his **D/I/C.** Before hiring, it became a strict rule to do a **DISC** assessment.

On the other hand, and in spite of what I have said in the previous chapter, many, many organizations still hire with no idea of human behavior patterns. The problem in a few non-profit groups (NGOs or Non-Governmental Organizations) I have seen has come in the selection of a board of directors. When the Executive Officer's strategy is to go out into the community and select confident and 'successful' people with their own businesses and their own wealth—he might end up with directors who are all strong **D's.** Why is that a problem? After all, a **D** 'gets things done,' right? Think, though, about a board's role. It needs to strategically direct an entire organization, true. But it also needs to go out into the community and talk to people with money and raise funds . . . get people to show up at their fund-raising events . . . encourage many to participate as volunteers in their projects and programs. Now imagine a board with directors who are all **D's**—not particularly people-oriented, not particularly patient, and who do not particularly use their verbal communication abilities to great advantage! How will the Board perform its given role? And what if, in another scenario, the Executive Officer ends up with all strong **I** board members? Or too many people displaying a strong **S**? You see now how any leader—and any organization—can benefit from an understanding of the patterns of human behavior in order to achieve the organization's goals. You might also detect a few excellent reasons to have a **DISC**-diverse team!

While it is true that you cannot pre-assign a behavior style to a child (the child is just going to be who he or she is going to be), you now also grasp the benefits of understanding each other's behavior patterns and styles, so that you can support, guide, interact, get along and communicate optimally as a family . . . whether it is a work organization or your real family.

Plans, and How Each Style Sets and Gets Goals

I hope you have seen how useless it would be to have this knowledge of patterns in human behavior unless you also have a plan or a strategy to apply it for improvements in yourself, in your business interactions, and in your personal relationships. 'Intellectual' understanding without a corresponding action is not powerful for you.

I told the story of The Interrupter, who saw interruptions she made triggered by her natural impatience. She was a strong **D**. Another of her **D** traits helped her make dramatic improvements—that of being strongly task-oriented. That preferred focus helped her buckle down and fairly easily create a task list for herself in view to erasing her 'bad' habits of interruption and impatience. She needed little to no assistance in creating and adhering to her plan. She did the follow-through all on her own, without prompting by anyone else.

I appreciate that not everyone is wired to create their own plan—or to undertake and complete it with success all on their own. And I say this because I understand the **DISC** patterns!

For instance, I had a desire to create this book for you. I am an **I-S** style, as I've said. Think about what you know about each of these two styles. How would I manage to map out, sit and focus on the writing of it and publish a book within a desired deadline possessing these styles?

My **I** doesn't like to 'map out' things because that is sitting and planning something (a task)—the **I** would rather just dream about and 'envision' the finished book. My **S** side wants plenty of time to think about the project before starting to write a word. My **I** aspect has short focus on any project and is not a good finisher—but the **S** aspect is, if only I could get it started! Both aspects are people-oriented—not task-focused—so writing a book (a big, big task) could well have been a passing fancy rather than a real outcome that I achieved.

Knowing my own behavior style in **DISC** terms, I knew that I'd need help staying accountable to the project and the deadlines—and even outlining it out coherently to get a good start. Knowing myself, I shopped around, so to speak, for that assistance:

1. keeping me on my *pre-announced schedule* of production and
2. keeping me *focused on a task* that I set for myself

Those are two things I naturally would have 'trouble' with, given my **style**. My behavior patterns haven't made me a clock- or calendar-watcher, so I might miss deadlines, or just not realize how much time is going by without me making the progress I had promised myself. I am also less task-focused than many people, and a book is . . . a task! Getting help was crucial if I was going to be serious about completing this book for you within a reasonable amount of time. My wife's support was primary, then someone watching the writing schedule came next—making sure I wrote 'writing time and goals' into my agenda and actually sat and did it. And here is the result.

Would a **D** have gotten to publication sooner? Maybe! My ultimate goal, though, was 'publish my book this year.' How you get yourself to the achievement of your own goal will be in good part about understanding your **DISC** styles and taking actions to gently, for the length of the project at hand, shift or adapt your style as needed to reach the goal.

What type of support or assistance do you need—whether you are doing a new project, striving to achieve a new goal like making a personal change, or something else important to you? Here are some hints.

- Strong **D's:** If you don't like *imposed instructions,* that is a reason why you need to write out your own! You **D's** are not much for following *imposed* or *detailed* guidelines, rules or processes, so you might be resistant to following a ready-made plan that you are given by someone else, just in terms of willingly doing the action items each day.

Jot down the highlights of your own process so that it is personalized, and have someone turn it into a daily To-Do list for you. Then? It's up to you to follow your own plan (just like our Interrupter did)!

- Strong **I's:** If you are more people-oriented than task-focused, you will need someone else to help keep you on target with your plan. You might even need someone to write your whole plan out for you in the first place, as you talk through it from start to finish. Get someone unlike you who is process- and task-focused (like a **C**) to give you a phone call or text you daily to remind you of today's action item or deadline.

- Strong **S's:** Your issue will be to firmly decide on one single change or course of action you believe would benefit you. Study it to death if you want, but you'll need to remind yourself that preparing for change is not the same as *making* a change! Also firmly decide on one, single, simple step-by-step plan which gradually takes you to your new desired place. You'll need your supportive partner to help you avoid procrastinating and just dive in daily to do the action items listed in your plan. Who can help you when you are procrastinating? Someone with whom you have a strong friendship of trust. Someone who knows that you are a strong finisher—but not a good starter!

- Strong **C's:** If you have identified one trait of your strong **C** that you honestly conclude is holding you back in some way, make a change! Don't plan it to death, because you ultimately just want a step-by-step process like our Interrupter's, which you can stick to day after day until you achieve the goal. Who can help you when you nit-pick and try to over-analyze either the plan itself or your progress? Maybe a **D** whom you trust—and who is task-oriented like you and somewhat reserved just like you, but who is also quicker to 'just jump in'—can be your 'second.' A **D** might be so impatient with your details and analytical side, that he (abruptly) pulls you back on course so that you move forward. That would be a good thing! Agree to report in daily or weekly to the **D** about what you have done.

Helping You Help Others

Keep in mind that this new **DISC** knowledge will *help you help others* in many ways. When any of the people I have described above come to you for support in achieving their goal by follow-ing their plan, what can you do? Understand their natural, usual behaviors, first of all. What is their **DISC** profile? From that, you add your observations of what keeps that person from following through. Not following through can start very early in this process! It can mean that your friend the strong **I** only says he is going to do this-or-that, and then moves to the next shiny thing in front of him. He never gets started even deciding what the change he desires to make—not without your nudge! Your friend the strong **C** might fall deep into so much analysis of what to do, how to do it, and then overanalyze if he actually did it—that he, too, is likely to spin his wheels without you. That friendly **S** who wants your help is a strong finisher, too, and you know this; his challenge is that he is not a fast starter, so again your support and nudging is essential to getting his plan for change launched.

You can position yourself in any interaction so that 1) you address others' strengths and minimize the focus on any of their weaknesses and 2) others get support from strengths you have that they do not.

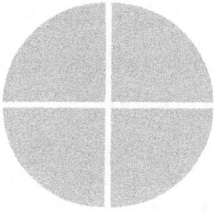

Conclusion

IN PRESENTING human behavior through the four styles called **DISC**, I have sidestepped presenting the theory and the science behind this method for understanding yourself and others. In my view, science and theory are not what we need today! Our brains are stuffed with facts and figures, but they are not what we need. We need a practical, hands-on, understandable process that is applicable to our current relationships and interactions. We need something we can *use now*.

I believe that with the **DISC** explanation of human behavior, you have a complete, powerful and infinitely applicable method for understanding yourself and others.

The **DISC** allows you to make small, momentary shifts in your own behavior easily whenever you need to interact and communicate better with someone of a different style from yours.

When a whole team or family learns the **DISC**, you have a

great tool. It gives you a common language from shared knowledge between two or more individuals living or working together and needing to get along and understand each other better.

The **DISC** allows each of you to look at your own profile and position amongst the four styles—with all the traits, motivations, strengths, weaknesses, tendencies and behaviors that you display—and decide all on your own which behaviors need elimination, modification, or simply more awareness on your part. It is a great tool for understanding others. It is a great tool for initiating personal growth in yourself.

Knowledge helps you decide what to minimize and what to push to the forefront in any given situation. And that is a lesson in and of itself: *Behavior is situational. Behavior is adjusted according to the context. Behavior is moldable* . . . by you, once you have awareness.

In my consulting practice, I have seen lightbulbs go on over people's heads once they realize what their own **DISC** style is. Likewise, when the style of those near and dear to them, or the style of those with whom they work, becomes clear to them, another lightbulb goes off.

Relationships are not about expecting others to be like us—not once we understand each other from the **DISC** perspective. That is why I can say that humans share the search for oneness with the greater family of man. Relationships are all about your awareness of how we are different, but more than that, how we are alike. We all want the same thing: To be loved. To be understood. To be heard. To be valued.

DISC gets us all closer to achieving that goal.

Answer Key
for the Quizzes

About the 'D', Jim - "Can you go back into the story of Jim and underscore the descriptive words and phrases that show how he is behaving from a purely **D** style?"

- dynamic
- get-it-done
- impatient in long, drawn-out meetings
- long conversations and inactivity are not his style
- loves long to-do lists of things to do on his own

About the 'I', Lizbet - "Can you go back to the story about Lizbet and underscore the descriptive words and phrases that tell us she is behaving from a purely I style?"

- energetic
- creative
- chatty
- extended family and all her friends are important to her
- gets along harmoniously
- time for fun
- no eye on the clock

Chapter 7, Quick Quiz

About the 'S', Edoardo - "Can you go back to the story about Edoardo and underscore the descriptive words and phrases that tell us he is behaving from a purely **S** pattern?"

- active, but never seems in any kind of rush
- volunteer; lend a hand; help
- doesn't know how to say 'No'
- connected from the heart
- enjoys people
- connects with shared values, friendly people and the chance to serve

Chapter 8, Quick Quiz

About the '**C**', Andrei - "Can you go back to the story about Andrei and underscore the descriptive words and phrases that tell us he is behaving from a purely **C** pattern?"

- excelling in science, math, logic and research
- forensic biology and forensic accounting
- model student
- interested in school
- prepared
- attention to his personal grooming
- trying to be invisible
- strength at studying and preparing for tests
- nervous and shy around people

Quiz on Your Understanding, preceding Chapter 9

Here are the answers you should/could have written.

1. The two styles that are fast-paced: *D/Dominant and I/Influential*

2. Which of those fast-paced styles is so fast, we might call it a 'whirlwind' pace? *I/Influential*

3. Name the two styles that are people-oriented: *I/Influential and S/Steady*

4. Of those styles, which one is more likely to invest in long-term relationship development? *S/Steady*

5. As described, which style is the most:

C/Conscientiousness - Quiet and reserved, even a loner
I/Influence - Talkative and gregarious
S/Steadiness - Emotional (at least visibly)
D/Dominance - 'Get it done' oriented

6. Can you give 4 or more 'memory jogging words' (words starting in the letter **D** for the Dominance style, etc.) for the **D, I, S** and **C** styles?

D: directive, domineering, dynamic, decisive, daring . . .
I: influential, inspiring, impetuous, involved, interested . . .
S: steady, supportive, status quo, service, sweet . . .
C: conscientious, correct, cognitive, critical thinker, consistent . . .

7. Can you name the two styles that are happy to follow rules and procedures, processes and instructions? *S/Steady and C/Conscientious*

8. Which are the two styles more likely to display reserve than the others? *C/Conscientious and S/Steady*

9. Which style is the opposite of the **S**/Steadiness style? *D/Dominant.* Name two ways they are opposites. *D is decisive, while S is not. S loves people and relationship-building, while D does not.*

10. Which style is the opposite of the **C**/Conscientious style? *I/Influential.* Name two ways they are opposites. *C would rather be alone, while I's prefer lots of people around. I's hate rules and procedures, while C's thrive on them.*

Quiz on Your Observations, preceding Chapter 10

Contrary to the other quizzes, I provide no answers here! You are the one who knows these people much, much better by now. It is up to you and your abilities to observe and understand your style and that of others. Take some time and write down answers that occur about each of these people.

List at least four people who are closest to you. They can be family, friends, coworkers, business partners—as you like. Write their first names down in a list like mine on the next page.

As an example, I will use the four individuals who helped me present each of the four styles, plus a fifth person I know.

1. Jim   fast-paced   **D**/Dominant   **D/I**
2. Lizbet   fast-paced   I/Influential   **I/S**
3. Edoardo   moderately paced **S**/Steady   **S/C**
4. Andrei   slow-paced   **C**/Conscientious   **C/D**
5. Guido   fast-paced   **D**/Dominant   **D/?**

After each name, write whether this person is fast-paced or (moderate) slow-paced.

Think about each one's single or strongest behavioral style right now. If you could only choose one behavior style for each person, which one would it be? Write it now, as I have on my list.

If you have two or more people on your list of the same predominant **DISC** style, like I do, can you name two ways that they are different from each other?

Lastly, indicate what you think their dominant pair of styles might be—just from your observations.

Resources

Print Books about DISC

The Personality Compass, by Diane Turner and Thelma Greco, 1998, Element Books, Inc.

Taking Flight! Master the DISC Styles to Transform Your Career, Your Relationships . . . Your Life, by Merrick Rosenberg and Daniel Silvert, 2013, Pearson Education Inc., publishing as FT Press.

The 4-Dimensional Manager—DISC Strategies for Managing Different People in the Best Ways, by Julie Straw, 2002, Inscape Publishing, Inc.

Communication Skills Magic - Improve Your Relationships and Productivity through Better Understanding Your Personality Style and the Personality Styles of Those Around You, by E.G. Sebastian, 2010, Timshel Publishing.

I'm Stuck, You're Stuck—Break Through to Better Work Relationship and Results by Discovering Your DISC Behavioral Style, by Tom Ritchey with Alan Axelrod, 2002, Inscape Publishing, Inc.

Positive Personality Profiles—"D-I-S-C-over" Personality Insights to Understand Yourself . . . and Others!, by Robert A. Rohm, PhD, 1993, 2000, Personality Insights, Inc.

Assessments

DISC Assessment www.thediscpersonalitytest.com

DISC Assessment http://www.discoveryreport.com

DISC Assessment https://discprofile.com

John Maxwell Leadership Assessment, http://store.johnmax-well.com/Maxwell-Leadership-Assessment_p_1065.html

360-Degree Feedback
https://www.echospan.com/360-degree-feedback.asp

Myers-Briggs Type Indicator—MBTI
https://www.mbtionline.com

Strong Interest Inventory
https://www.cpp.com/en-US/Products-and-Services/Strong

StrengthsFinder—CliftonStrengths
https://www.gallupstrengthscenter.com

About the Author

Abdulbaset Turkistani originally trained and worked as an electrical engineer (and later as an instrument engineer) in the petrochemical industry. Since those days, he has been active as a trainer, entrepreneur, public speaker, and corporate training manager. He is an ICF-certified coach and a member of the International Coaching Federation. Currently, Abdul is a Training Manager with National Petrochemical Corporation (NATPET). Abdul is also a business partner with the Inscape/John Wiley & Sons, Inc. publishing house, which distributes the DiSC assessment programs.

For generations, Abdul and his family have lived in Saudi Arabia, and in his leisure time, you'll find him jogging, traveling internationally on vacation trips, or just curled up with a good book.

Discovering the DISC patterns of human behavior (notably his own) changed Abdul's life—at home with his wife and children, and in his interactions with work partners and clients—and it is to share this life-changing, eye-opening information with as many people as he can that he has written this book.

For speaking and training events,
please contact Abdul at **turkistani@discarabic.com**

www.ingramcontent.com/pod-product-compliance
Lightning Source LLC
Chambersburg PA
CBHW031145270326
41931CB00006B/154